THE
MULTIGENERATIONAL
SALES TEAM

THE
MULTIGENERATIONAL
SALES TEAM

Harness the Power of New Perspectives to
Sell More, Retain Top Talent, and
Design a High-Performing Workplace

Warren Shiver and David Szen

CAREER
PRESS
Wayne, NJ

THE MULTIGENERATIONAL SALES TEAM
Edited by Jodie Brandon
Typeset by Diana Ghazzawi
Cover design by Rightly Designed
Cover illustration by whitehoune/adobe
Printed in the U.S.A.

To order this title, please call toll-free 1-800-CAREER-1 (NJ and Canada: 201-848-0310) to order using VISA or MasterCard, or for further information on books from Career Press.

The Career Press, Inc.
12 Parish Drive
Wayne, NJ 07470
www.careerpress.com

Library of Congress Cataloging-in-Publication Data

CIP Data Available Upon Request.

Acknowledgments

This book is not only a collaborative effort between the authors, but also between two incredible team members who have collectively spent more than 1,000 hours researching, surveying, interviewing, writing, editing, and project managing this entire effort. In addition to being two wonderful colleagues, Erica Abt and Kelsey Peusch have proven themselves to be true partners in this effort, and we thank them for their significant contributions to this work.

We have both benefited from working with an incredibly talented team at Symmetrics Group, many of whom have contributed their ideas and experiences, which have helped this book take shape. We would also like to thank John Willig of Literary Services, Inc., who believed in our project, and the team at Career Press, who brought this book to you.

We are greatly appreciative of our clients, sellers, and sales leaders who willingly shared their time, experiences, and lessons learned. They include Mo Bunnell, Kenneth Burton, Chris Dessi, Drew Frick, Theresa Highsmith, Eric Middleton, Larry Nettles, Alan Powell, Lisa Redekop, Steve Richard, Mike Rosenberg, Rosann Spiro, Evan Steiner, Dave Stillman, Mitch Touart, Ian Walch, Larry Walker, and Ewelina Wojnowska.

Thank you also to Mark Hawn, David Hamme, David Mast, and Michael Merlin for their support of the authors and our firm.

We would also like to thank our families for supporting our professional passion and the late nights and weekends consumed by this project. Thank you to Paige, Avery, and Morgan Shiver, as well as Brandi and Olivia Szen. A special thank you to Leslie and Robert Rothberg for literally saving Warren's life thanks to Leslie's kidney donation. Leslie, you are truly a hero.

We are passionate about the selling profession and working with sellers and sales leaders across all generations. Our hope is that this book serves as a guide to help you integrate generational awareness into your sales process, reinforce it with your sales leadership, and utilize it to strengthen organizational capabilities.

Good reading and good selling.

Contents

Introduction

We are about to deliver a presentation at an annual sales conference for a large U.S.–based energy company. As we stand on stage and look out over an audience of five hundred people, we are struck by what we see: In the large ballroom there is a sea of individual sellers, sales leaders, support staff, and executives—a melting pot of age groups represented. Some sellers appear to have a few decades of experience, whereas the senior leadership team all appear to be in the latter years of their careers, and there are pockets of youth all clustered together around the room. There are people who have undoubtedly been through dozens of annual sales kickoff meetings and others who are encountering this type of production for the first time.

This team, like many teams, must find ways to succeed and achieve revenue goals despite palpable differences in the way they work, sell, and communicate. We both think for a moment: Will our messages resonate with the audience? Will the material be relevant to everyone in the room? Will some of these people connect faster with us and our presentation and speaking styles? How can we be safe with our words and stories so that we do not abandon anyone? What would we do if we had to lead such a team in this generational melting pot?

The composition of generations in the workforce today is different than ever before. In the consulting industry, your authors have the benefit of working with companies from a variety of industries, sizes, and geographies. In our role as consultants, we have worked with hundreds of organizations over the past five years, specifically in the area of sales effectiveness. Increasingly, we witness firsthand the demographic changes in sales teams, in buyer profiles, and in companies overall, including our own.

The concept of generational diversity is not new. A voluminous amount of quality information is available on the different generations, in the form of books, videos, workshops, and whitepapers. Also based on a quick search of Amazon.com, there are currently more than 16,000 books on the topic of sales, 32,000 on the topic of leadership, and several thousand books on the topic of generational concepts. Even if you had the time, this would be a rather aggressive reading list. In *The Multigenerational Sales Team*, however, we take a unique approach and look at the intersection of these three topics: sales, leadership, and generational concepts. In our research for this book, we conducted more than 60 interviews and surveyed more than 140 sales professionals on the relevance and importance of this very topic, but we have yet to see any material content that addresses how sales leadership and generational concepts intersect in the professional world today.

In all of the existing books on sales and generations, there is little research on how sales organizations should prepare to effectively leverage the skills and talents of multiple generations. While we recommend Cam Marston's books,[1] which are focused on techniques to sell to and manage a team of Millennials, in this book we will focus on how to optimize a multigenerational sales team and provide you with the following:

1. An improved understanding of generational diversity and, more importantly, how generations typically interact with one another.

2. Insights on how generational differences impact customer interactions.

3. Advice for sales leaders to adapt their coaching style and frequency to account for generational differences.

4. Recommendations to apply these concepts in your sales team and organization in order to improve performance.

5. Advice for both sellers and sales managers on how to thrive and lead in a multigenerational environment.

1

The Generational Imperative

"Each generation imagines itself to be more intelligent than the one that went before it, and wiser than the one that comes after it."

—George Orwell, English novelist, essayist, journalist, and critic (1903–1950)

The composition of today's workforce is complex and will continue to evolve over the next 10 to 15 years. Having read our fair share of materials on the topic, we felt an overwhelming sense of negativity associated with the topic. The majority of articles spoke little about how to overcome the obstacle, instead keying in on annoying behaviors that seemed to stereotype each generation. It is important to recognize that there are many positive impacts from the generational mash-up affecting the workplace. A great example is a well-known, global coffee company. Starbucks employs a wide mix of ages, with store associates, managers, district managers, and regional leadership representing a broad swath of age groups. Employees and customers of Starbucks call this workplace their "third place between work and home,"[1] which is no doubt a result of the company's effort to make their employees and customers feel a certain way. As part of these efforts, the company celebrates generational, cultural, and lifestyle differences. Starbucks clearly understands the power of harnessing generational differences and allowing people to be who they are while at work. Try to resist the urge to look at generational differences as only challenging or frustrating. There are many examples of companies that have embraced generational differences and have achieved extremely positive outcomes as a result.

You may be surprised to know that Millennials now represent the second largest generation in the workforce today. According to the Department of Labor Population Survey, the breakdown of the generations in the U.S. employed civilian workforce in 2015[2] was:

- 51.5 million people, or roughly 35 percent Millennials.

- 63.9 million people, or roughly 43 percent Gen X.

- 29.9 million people, or roughly 20 percent Baby Boomers.

- 3.5 million people, or roughly 2 percent Silent Generation.

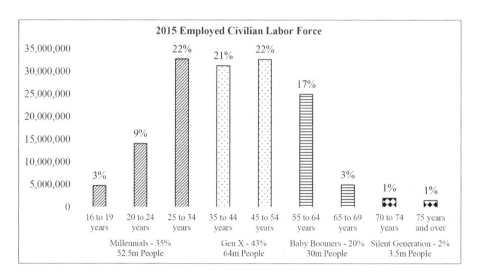

As generational groupings can sometimes be nebulous, for the purpose of this book we will reference the generations as follows:

- Baby Boomers were born 1946–1964 and are ages 52 to 71 in 2016.

- Gen Xers were born 1965–1979 and are ages 37 to 51 in 2016.

- Millennials were born 1980–2000 and are ages 16 to 36 in 2016.

These numbers are changing every day. Currently more than 10,000 Baby Boomers retire from the workforce daily, which translates to more than 4 million Baby Boomers per year.[3] The trends are easy to understand: Despite data that shows Baby Boomers are working into later stages of life, their representation in the workforce is rapidly shrinking, Gen X representation will remain fairly stable over the next decade, and Millennial representation in the workforce will continue to increase. No matter how you look at the numbers, a study conducted by Ernst & Young highlights the current demographic reality: by 2025 Millennials will represent 75 percent of the workforce.[4] Welcome to the Generational Imperative.

So, what makes these demographic changes so imperative that they require immediate action? First, we are losing our most experienced workers. Second, the numbers are dictating a need for a real strategy in order to keep the sales engine running. Senior executives and investors will not give a sales leader a "pass" to miss revenue targets while they train and develop new sales talent. Without question, none of us in sales or leadership positions can sit back and wait to see how it all unfolds.

Some of you may be thinking, "This is not new, and it has happened before." You are correct. Generational differences have existed in the workforce since the early 1900s, starting with the Industrial Revolution and the major transition from a rural, agrarian society to an urban, industrial society. Another major generational transition took place in the 1950s and 1960s with rapid changes in technology and transportation: from radio to television, black and white to color TV, computers and electronic communications, copiers, and so forth. We went to the moon, popularized rock 'n' roll music, and adapted to significant cultural shifts. In the workforce, workers and employers both still prized stability and loyalty. For example, the Bureau of Labor Statistics calculated that in 1960, Americans had been with their current employer for 22.5 years.[5] In 2014, the Bureau of Labor Statistics released the results of an Employee Tenure Survey that stated that the median number of years workers had been with their current employer was 4.6 years.[6] That translates to a drop in nearly 18 years of tenure over the last 50 years!

Looking back at our personal experiences, we see many of the differences between the workplace of today compared to 40 or 50 years ago. David's father worked for AT&T for 38 years. It is the only job he ever had. He started with NY Telephone, which was folded into AT&T in the 1980s and his first job was to climb telephone poles, after which he ultimately moved into a position installing and servicing large enterprise-level phone systems. David's family looked forward to the annual AT&T summer picnic. AT&T held these events at large amusement parks or in large public parks, and they involved cooking out, family fun, games, activities, and "rubbing elbows." David's father was more of a blue-collar worker, but the executives and senior leaders attended these events as well. It was a celebration of all things AT&T. Employees were recognized for years of service, promotions, retirement, and outstanding service accomplishments; the culture was defined by loyalty and longevity at all levels within the organization. David knew many of the families, and it was normal to spend time together, take family trips together, laugh, cry, and consider themselves part of the extended AT&T family. The unwritten contract between the company and employee was totally different from what we see today. AT&T employees in that era did not leave the corporate "family" until it was time to say goodbye, which usually meant retirement. During David's father's career, workplace expectations included loyalty, years of service, long-term thinking, promotions, stability, benefits, retirement plans, and family.

Similarly, Warren's father began work with Newcomb & Boyd, an Atlanta-based consulting engineering firm, while finishing his education at Georgia Tech in 1959. He remained with the firm for 40 years, until his passing in 1999. Like a smaller version of AT&T, Newcomb & Boyd was a professional "family" and all of the leaders of the firm ("partners") were promoted from within, usually after 10 to 20 years with the firm.

Since that era, some incredible things occurred in the United States. The U.S. population from 1950 to 2000 doubled, and the so did the size of the workforce.[7] In 1950, the workforce population was 62 million people. In 2000, the workforce population was more than 140 million people.[8] The social contract between employee and employer changed dramatically as well. Employers enriched benefit programs, healthcare, retirement plans, and earning potential. Employees expected these things from employer to employer but some reshaping of the "loyalty definition" was well underway. A technology boom bubbled at the surface, new companies emerged, and by the 1980s and 1990s, the majority of the workers were Baby Boomers and the inflow of new workers from Gen X increased. In this era, senior leaders and experienced veterans who lead the workplace in 2016 were just beginning their professional careers.

Because both of us represent Gen X, we have also experienced these workplace changes directly. In David's case, he went to high school and college in the 1980s: no cell phones, no PCs, answering machines, no social media, no DVRs, no CDs, the Sony Walkman, the boom box, and the space shuttle. He started his professional career in sales, cold-calling businesses on the phone more than 100 times daily in order to set appointments for outside sellers. They called it sales: It was telemarketing with a small chance to survive, but his first bosses and influencers were either Baby Boomers or older. Work was still a game of "pay your dues" and "listen to your bosses, who have been here longer than you." It was truly an "old school" environment: Sellers either dialed the phones or knocked on doors and captured results in paper files. As David's career progressed, he was thrilled when he was able to start faxing documents to colleagues. Soon enough, computers started to arrive on the scene, but unless you were a technologist, or selling within a high-tech industry, computers were not yet useful. David had a cellphone but did not use it for anything besides making phone calls, if that, as reception was extremely unreliable. At the time, job-hopping was frowned upon and David knew that he had to pay his dues to climb any ladder. The pace of change was accelerating but manageable and interpersonal differences were not mountainous. These were the "good old days," and it was only 25 years ago.

For Warren, it was a similar experience, but having entered the workforce a decade later, the pace of change accelerated. Warren began his career in management consulting just as portable (laptop) personal computers were being adopted. (In fact, his new hire training consisted of one of the last start groups to go through COBOL training. Bonus points if you can define that acronym.[9]) At his firm, the expectation was to advance within the firm and work your way up to partner. But with the new millennium, the dotcom era arrived and with it startup companies, IPOs, job-hopping to the "new new thing,"[10] and the rapid decline of the monolithic corporation—and with it, the loss of guaranteed career paths with a single organization. Warren's career has mimicked many of these trends, as he has since worked for more than five different companies and has started his own firm, Symmetrics Group.

We are not alone in saying that more has changed in technology and the world in the last 10 years than in the previous one thousand years. As Eric Schmidt and Jonathan Rosenberg of Google write in their book, *How Google Works*, "the pace of change is accelerating."[11] The generation that was born in the late 1980s and early 1990s never knew a world without the majority of what we have today and take it for granted. (As an example, just watch a 2-year-old navigate an iPad or a 6-year-old teach his or her grandparents how to use a smartphone. Interestingly, Apple sells 1,000 devices every couple minutes.[12]) The differences between people entering the workplace today and those who have been around for 20 years or more are significant, and technology is one of the significant drivers of these differences.

· ·

Exploring Generational Differences

Just how big are the differences today? Certain expectations have been created that seem to perpetuate the generational divide. Let's take a look at a few scenarios in order to grasp the depth of the Generational Imperative and its impact within sales organization.

Expectations for Open Communication With the C-Suite (Titles Like CEO, CFO, COO)

In an interview with a Millennial seller named Mitch Touart, who currently works at a startup company named Gladly headquartered in Silicon Valley, we learned that it is not uncommon for Millennials to expect access and open dialogue with their leadership team. Mitch told us that, though cultures that promote this type of transparency can be great, "the dialogue can become hostile quickly, meaning the culture can become really stressful and siloed, because the Millennial seller sometimes divulges more than sellers from other generations." If we had asked for access to the CEO in 1993, our bosses would have looked at us like we had four heads and then put us on watch as "problem children." Today, however, these are normal conversations that happen and are even expected in some companies. As authors, we have seen C-Suite communication evolve from a "need to know" to an "open door" policy over the past 25 years.

Expectations for Longevity in a Role or Within an Organization

A quick look back in time points to major shifts in attitudes toward tenure with a company. As referenced above, professionals in the 1960s spent more than 15 more years, on average, with their employer than professionals do today. We continue to see that it is perfectly normal if professionals have numerous roles or companies on their resume before they turn 30. Many seem to have a "try this out" philosophy, which leaves hiring managers and sales leaders confused and frustrated. David Stillman and Steve Richard, who lead a Washington, DC–based company called Vorsight, illustrated this well. They had a Millennial "up and comer" who the organization was developing because of the seller's promising future. To ensure this star employee would continue to be engaged at their company, Vorsight promoted the seller to a training department role, to challenge him and allow to him learn a new part of the business. After nine months in the promoted role, the seller quit and told his boss, "I learned everything that I needed to learn in these nine months." David and Steve could not believe this star employee could not see the opportunities that lay ahead that would allow him to continue to learn and grow within the organization. The Millennial mindset is more focused on "being whatever you want to be"—not necessarily loyalty and longevity to a company. This represents a change for organizations and employees alike.

Expectations for Career Growth and Ability to Advance Quickly

We have had the pleasure of spending a number of years as sales professionals and leaders within several environments, including inside sales, enterprise-level outside sales, professional services sales, entrepreneurs, and so on. In the past, many of those seeking sales roles took these roles for the earning potential. Today, many entering sales positions see the role as a "stepping stone" and quickly look to define their next step, either inside or outside of the company. In our research, we found that a higher percentage of Millennials would rather hold multiple roles over two years and strive for proficiency, compared to the other generations that prefer to hold a single role and strive for mastery. Increasingly, senior sales leaders are bothered by this mindset unless their sales team/roles are truly an entry-level proposition. Companies need sellers who come onboard, learn, build a book of business and relationships with clients, and stay in the role. Unfortunately, many people focus on what is next and not the role they are in, and they usually fail. In starting our careers, if we had requested an open-door policy and frequently asked what else we could do within the company, our bosses might have helped us find the elevators to exit the building. Today, this dialogue occurs during the interview process.

Expectations for the Boundaries Between Business and Social Time

In our early professional careers, social time was called happy hour after work. We did not have smartphones, iPads, Facebook, Snapchat, and so forth, so the temptation to engage in personal life during work hours was limited to communication with coworkers and the occasional personal phone call. Mostly, there was a clear line between business and social time. Today, there is always an opportunity for "social time," not to mention a multitude of channels and mediums for social interaction.

Companies must now decide what message to send when it comes to social interaction during work hours. Are employees allowed to be on Facebook during the day? Can they Tweet? Can they read news on any site returned by Google? Should we set restrictions or policies? Will we run the risk of sounding like communists? Today, even in interviews, candidates ask about the company's culture and approach on policies for these types of decisions.

. . . .

Positive Impacts From the Generations in Today's Workforce

Now that we have identified several impacts of the Generational Imperative, let's highlight some of the positives that result from the generational mix in today's workforce.

We Still Have Experienced People in Key Roles (Baby Boomers and Gen X)

This is great news for worried leaders. The most tenured employees can help us teach new employees and first-time team leaders, and ease the transition associated with large books of business. This typically requires a defined mentoring program to extract the wealth of knowledge that has been accrued over time. Hundreds of wins, and potentially even more losses, provide experiential awareness that younger generations simply lack.

Millennials Bring Several Exceptional Talents to the Workplace

This generation has grown up with technology, which drives a significantly smaller learning curve when it comes to new technology and applications. Millennials typically understand social media and its place in company branding, tend to work collaboratively in groups, can interact with multiple technologies at a time, excel at research, are quick learners, and have a healthy respect for work/life balance. Millennials also are highly educated and have incredible skills at their disposal just waiting to be honed. In 1992, only 30 percent of college-age individuals in the United States (25 to 34 years old) obtained a post-secondary degree (associate's, bachelor's, or graduate). By 2013, this number had increased to 47 percent.[13] What they lack in experiential learning, they make up for in theory, and they are poised to make their mark by putting what they've learned into practice.

Effective Training Offers Growth Potential and Great Future Benefits

So we have new people to teach? Great! That means we have to design sales training that prepares people for success. This makes jobs easier to market. Plus, our research supports the assumption that sales professionals seek opportunities to work for organizations with a well-defined learning path. Later in this book, we'll explore data from our survey that measures the importance of various factors for sellers contemplating a new sales job. Not surprisingly, Millennials ranked "compelling career path" third, only after compensation-related benefits, and "robust training program" was listed in the top eight (out of 15) factors for all three generations. Get a double benefit from this and utilize your experienced sellers in designing the training so that you know you are teaching relevant material in a relevant way.

As you consider how to address the Generational Imperative within your own company and sales team, it is important to keep in mind what we call the Generational Golden Rules. In order to enable seamless communications, and to avoid making first impressions based solely on age or generational group, consider these guiding principles:

1. Many people break stereotypes. Not everyone within a certain age range is identical. Keep an open mind and leave room for people to surprise you. Generational characteristics inform our behaviors but are written in pencil, not in stone.

2. People are a complex blend of personality, social styles, ways of thinking, communication preferences, and motivations. Generational differences are simply an additional layer to

include as we consider the motivations and behaviors of our colleagues.

3. Generations have been influenced by one another and can take on characteristics of their leaders from other generations. Our first bosses are typically from an older generation, so naturally many have picked up some of their tendencies and characteristics.

4. Keep generational differences as neutral as possible to avoid flare-ups up to the point of no return—especially in sales, sales leadership, and coaching.

5. The workplace, and sales specifically, will never be the same again. For those of us grounded in prior eras, we should let it go, accept that this is a different time, and focus on what we can embrace to make the best of generational behaviors and preferences in the workforce today.

Now that we have identified the impacts and benefits of generational diversity in the workplace, let's turn our attention to the world of sales.

The Impact of Generations on Sales Organizations

As authors and for our broader team, we all love sales. We have decades of experience together working in roles covering sales, sales leadership, and sales transformations, as well as training and development. We launched our company, Symmetrics Group, in 2010 with a sole focus on strengthening business-to-business sales organizations. Through our client work, we have had the privilege of working with numerous clients across many different industries and selling models to improve their performance. Sales growth is almost always high on the priority list for every company. In addition to revenue growth, other significant sales priorities are typically:

- Grow or maintain market share.
- Improve sales team productivity.
- Grow sales with existing customers.
- Launch new products or services.
- Win back lapsed customers from competitors.

These priorities tend to arrive back at the same starting point—companies must sell more of what they make or provide to the market—and each can be impacted by generational differences.

As we think about the generational makeup of sales organizations, increasingly sales teams are growing by hiring Millennials. Given that many of these are filled by recent college graduates in either their first or second role, we would expect to see many of them entering the workforce with degrees in marketing or sales. Yet, the number of colleges offering a formal degree in sales is significantly smaller than those that offer other majors that have a much lower volume of job opportunities tied to them. It seems we are educating our Millennials for the wrong fields, and it may be the reason that so many young people end up back in school for a master's degree in something they can actually get employed doing. As Brent Rasmussen, president of CareerBuilder North America, says, "There is a disconnect between the demand for sales skills in corporate America and the formal training available either through academic institutions or within companies themselves."[14]

It's not surprising that "an estimated 50 percent of college graduates start their career in sales. Very few of these graduates have any sales training when they enter the workplace and, as a result, the majority fail during their first year on the job," said Rosann Spiro, executive director of the Kelley School's Center for Global Sales Leadership and author of the best-selling text on sales management.[15] A study from Economic Modeling Specialists (a CareerBuilder company), shows that in 2013, there were twice as many colleges and universities in the United States that offer degrees in geology (559) compared with degrees in sales (274). Additionally, psychology degrees outpace sales degrees by six to one (1,571 schools offer psychology degrees in the United States). Comparing educational background and degrees to actual employment offerings some interesting (maybe disturbing) comparisons: "Sales-related fields account for 15,517,185 U.S. jobs compared to 167,728 in psychology-related fields (93:1 sales to psychology) and 94,696 in geology-related fields (164:1 sales to geology). In 2015, there were 678,968 job openings in sales-related fields compared to 8,698 jobs in psychology-related fields and 6,766 job openings in geology-related fields."[16] We expect the employment possibilities are even more challenging for many other degrees. These are alarming numbers, especially as those geologists fill roles that do not match their training.

As we will outline in this book, with increasing numbers of college graduates joining companies in sales positions, sales organizations are finding that they need to develop more formal training and development paths to equip their new hires to be successful in sales. Many companies are adapting and building sales development programs tailored to attract and retain Millennial talent while reducing their time to productivity, a topic that we will explore in Chapter 4 and Chapter 5.

Additionally, hiring managers must remember that ideal sales candidates may look different today than they did in the past. Mike Rosenberg, head of sales for Healthgrades, a U.S. company that provides information about physicians, hospitals, and healthcare providers with information on more than 3 million U.S. healthcare providers,[17] told us that his organization is flexible on the profile of sales candidates, and in fact, in the past he has hired both experienced and inexperienced candidates, which he believes has little correlation with success at his company; instead he looks for aptitude and a "likeability factor" that is hard to quantify or define. Today, experience and education are only a sliver of the selection process, and increasingly we are seeing soft skills outweigh traditional selling skills. We will further explore how sales organizations must adapt their recruiting and onboarding approach in Chapter 5.

To further illustrate how generational nuances impact sales, let's examine a few situations in which having a deeper understanding of generational differences and preferences may prove useful:

- Imagine a 28-year-old seller calling on a 56-year-old decision-maker.

- Imagine a remote employee who is learning sales and only sees their manager twice a year and communicates only by phone, text, or email.

- Imagine a brand new seller who has no formal training or sales experience calling on a high-value and longtime strategic account.

- Imagine a 47-year-old sales manager trying to manage a team of new young sellers and a few Baby Boomers.

- Imagine a 58-year-old seller with almost 30 years of sales experience calling on a 34-year-old decision-maker who wants to communicate via text instead of meeting in person.

- Imagine a sales team that is experiencing high turnover among new sellers because they have no prior sales experience or skills, and the sales leaders do not have the time to train these skills.

- Imagine a 56-year-old candidate looking for a new challenge in sales and the hiring managers can't help but think that the candidate will not be working for much longer.

What are the answers to all of these situations? Certainly there are numerous possibilities, but our takeaway is that now is the time to bridge the gap between generational differences and sales effectiveness. Next, in Chapter 2, we will introduce you to the generations in a more formal way. By defining each generation, and the characteristics which typify them, you will understand the differences between and among them and the many myths often associated with each generation. We will introduce you to the concept of "Generational Flexibility," which will ensure generational differences drive fewer issues between sellers, leaders, and in the buying process. Whether you are in sales, sales leadership, or other roles, we will provide you with a set of stories and examples that set an excellent foundation for understanding and adapting to the Generational Imperative affecting your career and organization.

2

Generational Definitions and Dispelling Common Myths

"The children now love luxury. They have bad manners [and] contempt for authority."

—Socrates, Greek philosopher (470–399 BC)

Meet Jason. Jason has held nine roles with the same consumer products company over the last 13 years. He rose to the level of vice president in his first four years and is the embodiment of a high performer. Jason currently oversees a sales team that manages some of the company's largest retail accounts which account for 45 percent of Central Garden's annual revenue.[1]

With the support of Central Garden's leadership team, Jason has invested heavily in his professional development, recently earning his MBA from a top-ranked business school. Jason enjoys tremendous loyalty from his sales team and has developed strong relationships at the highest levels within the company. Jason is climbing the corporate ladder yet continues to enjoy respect from his peers, who appreciate his professionalism, high business EQ (emotional quotient/intelligence), and strong work ethic. The proud father of two children, he is early to arrive at the office, travels 75 percent of his time, and puts in long hours. Somehow, he finds time to enjoy the kids and family and spend time in the great outdoors.

Can you guess Jason's generation? Baby Boomer? Gen X? Millennial? Your authors will be the first to admit that we made some assumptions and got it all wrong the first time we met Jason at a sales conference in 2012. He was already running a large part of the business as a vice president, and we expected a more seasoned professional purely based on his title. We failed at picking Jason out in the group since we were looking for a gray-haired individual with the appearance of several decades of experience. Jason quickly delighted us once we realized he was a strong, but young, professional leader doing exceptionally well in his high-profile role. These are easy mistakes to make. It's human nature. What's important is that we, as sellers, recognize when we are falling into a generational guessing game before it's too late. Being self-aware allows us to take note and contemplate how this may impact the way we engage with those around us.

In this chapter, we will introduce you to the three generations working simultaneously in today's selling environment, and we will outline a common set of descriptors and characteristics for each generation. Our goal is to assist readers in not only being able to identify an individual's generation but to provide a greater understanding of their preferences, tendencies, and perspectives. We certainly have not invented this data, but by being aware of what the data communicates, within the context for how we treat our colleagues and clients, our hope is to provide a competitive advantage for both individuals and companies alike.

. . . .

Defining the Generations

A quick Google search provides access to more than 200 million articles that in various ways describe the different generations. As many of you are already familiar with at least the outlines of the generations, we will focus on the crucial characteristics that are especially important with respect to sales and sales leadership. Our expertise is not in defining or redefining the generations, but in defining the impact generational differences have on the sales profession.

In order to define each generation, we will focus on the three generations that make up the majority of today's workforce. Please note that we will not be delving into the characteristics of the Traditionalists or the Silent Generation (born between 1901 and 1942), nor will touch on Generation Z (anyone born after 2000). Consider the following Generation Characteristics[2] table as a reference guide for understanding each generation.

	Millennial Born 1980-2000	Gen X Born 1965-1979	Baby Boomers Born 1945-1964
Key Influencers	Social Media Terrorism Financial Crisis Student Loan Debt	Dual-Income Families Single Parents Technology Boom and Bust Business Downsizing	Civil Rights Vietnam War Cold War Energy Crisis Space Travel
Key Descriptors	High Expectations Confident Sociable Technically Savvy Community-Oriented Want it now!	High Achievers Independent Balanced Pragmatic Family-Oriented Want it proven!	Personally Gratified Realists Traditional Mistrustful Equality-Oriented Want to make a difference!
Work Ethic	Ambitious Multi-Taskers Entrepreneurial	Efficient Self-sufficient Skeptical	Driven Workaholics Transformational
Focus	Global and Networked	Task and Results	Relationships and Results
Embrace of Generational Label	40%	58%	79%

. . . .

Generational Slices—Not the Whole Pie

People do not like to be unfairly judged by being a member of a group they *appear* to belong to, whether it's ethnic, religious, political, or geographic. Clearly defined generations have caused conflicts since the beginning of time. From Socrates to George Orwell, who was quoted as saying, "Each generation imagines itself to be more intelligent than the one that went before it and wiser than the one that comes after it,"[3] the ability to avoid applying broad stereotypes based on an individual's age, and generational cohort, is important, and being aware of the Generational Imperative will only help avoid what has been a topic of conflict for millennia.

Applied to age and one's place in a generational grouping, one might use a "whole pie" approach and assign broad sweeping characteristics and stereotypes to a single individual. Unfortunately, it's not that easy or straightforward. A person's place in life, as well as their unique experiences, can make certain generational characteristics more or less prominent. And as noted in the table on page 33, when it comes to Millennials, Pew Research has found that only 40 percent of adults ages 18 to 34 consider themselves part of the Millennial generation.[4] This is why we suggest considering a "generation slice" instead of applying the "whole pie" approach when identifying a particular individual.

There are a few important considerations when slicing a generation, including relationship status, work experience, career aspirations, family status, mortgage/rent, lifestyle, years to retirement, caring for their own parents, kids in college, saving for college, and debt. If you use a generation as a starting point, all of these attributes have an impact and may begin to blur the lines of a single generation. Let's illustrate this concept with a few examples.

Consider the Millennial generation, which includes a wide range of ages in today's workplace: people from 21 through 36 years of age. We do not see too many people in the professional world younger than 21, in fact, 23 to 25 is typical for most new hires. To be fair, as many Millennials seek master's degrees in lieu of a job market that is less than appealing, new hires are entering the workforce closer to 25 years of age. (According to Pew Research, "In 2009, the most recent data available, 27 percent of college-educated young adults had gone on to also complete an advanced degree."[5])

Compare the following two Millennials:

Millennial, Age 25	Millennial, Age 32
1st Professional role	4th Professional role
Master's Degree	Master's Degree
Single	Married
No children	One child
Apartment with a roommate (rents)	Owns 1st home (mortgage)
Lives for the weekend	Weekends include family and chores
Party nights	Date night once per month
Travel the world	Summer week at the beach
Happy to have a job	Looking for growth in a long-term career
Technology savvy	Technology savvy

Though these two individuals are both Millennials, they are very different individuals. Personal and professional differences will be apparent to their managers, their colleagues, and those they interact with outside the organization. They will place different levels of importance on work/life balance and for very different reasons. One probably would like to get home in order to balance family needs while the other has softball on Tuesday night, spin class on Wednesday, volunteer work on Thursday, and a social life kicking off on Friday, all of which is complicated by relationship drama and a constant desire to compare their life to that of their friend's carefully curated Instagram account. If you are 25 and feel that you were just unfairly characterized, you may "unlike" us but if you are in your 40s or older, you're probably laughing. One person has the pressure of a mortgage and is motivated by stability and financial reward, while the other may have the opportunity to move back home if their current job does not work out. According to recent research by the Pew Research Center, "In 2014, for the first time in more than 130 years, adults ages 18 to 34 were slightly more likely to be living in their parents' home than they were to be living with a spouse or partner in their own household."[6] This isn't always a choice but a result of the current working environment and a hamster wheel of rejection.

We must resist the urge to call out one generation over another in a derogatory fashion, especially when comparing people in the workplace. This may seem intuitive, but often an endearing remark, such as "Oh, those Millennials," can create a detrimental rift that is often hard to mend. Generational slicing points out that, even within a generation, external factors impact the characteristics and tendencies of the individual. When polled, only 40 percent of adults that actually fall under the "Millennial" cohort identify with the group, whereas 33 percent, mostly older Millennials, consider themselves part of the older generation, Gen X. Generational identity is actually the strongest among the Baby Boomer generation, with 79 percent considering themselves part of that generation.[7] In summary, whereas Millennials may have several things in common, they are not in the same place in life. In our experience, the 25-year-old Millennial will probably not be pleased to be compared to the 34-year-old Millennial, and vice versa.

We recently sat down with a 31-year-old seller who embodied the scenario above. We asked her what types of people have struggled in her sales role. Her answer cut deep, citing "older sales reps" as those having the hardest time. We asked her to define "older" and she said, "Over 45." Ouch. She went on to qualify the statement and began to speak about her own age group as well, but the comment wasn't lost on us. Given the context of our interaction, the comment stung but had no lasting implications on our relationship. Imagine, though, that instead of a one-time interview participant, this individual was a fellow colleague or a seller engaging a buyer. Contextualized, you can instantly feel the cringing effect of the comment.

This 31-year-old sales rep goes on to explain that she cannot believe that her own generation can't get it together and capitalize on the job. She displayed an utter disgust for the 20-somethings that fail in the role and told us that she spends no time with them at all professionally or socially. Recognizing that generational slices may more closely characterize an individual is an important realization. As you can imagine, if gone unnoticed, serious impacts will likely be felt among colleagues, between managers and direct reports, and when prospecting and serving customers.

Let's look at another example from the Baby Boomer generation. Next we will be comparing a 54-year-old Baby Boomer in a senior leadership role to a 61-year-old Baby Boomer in a strategic sales role.

Baby Boomer, Age 54	Baby Boomer, Age 61
Senior leader, 11 years in role	Strategic seller, 30+ years in role
30 direct reports	No direct reports
Reports to the CEO	Reports to a VP of sales
Married twice	Married for 36 years
3 children (ages 10, 13, 26)	2 children (ages 31, 34)
Saving for college	College years are over
15 years left to pay on a mortgage	Two mortgages paid off
Family vacations	Family vacations
Loyal to the company	Loyal to the company
Technology savvy	Tolerates technology
Needs to work 15+ more years	Could retire at any time
Wants more power within organization	Wants to be left alone
Works on vacation	Unplugs completely on vacation

We must resist the urge to say "those Baby Boomers" when we compare these two individuals. Again, they have much in common and would seem to work very well together because they identify with many of the same values. They mutually respect each other's tenure and experience in key roles. Our 54-year-old leader comes to work with the collective weight of the company and direct reports whereas the 61-year-old strategic seller is much more of an individual contributor who is motivated to "save the quarter" with a big sale. The younger Boomer must earn more to pay for college and the mortgage, causing him to spend at least two hours a day "switched on" during family vacations. The other gets away for two months per year for fun family vacations in a second home that is paid off. One is interested in the path for further growth and is open to a big opportunity if it comes along and the other just wants to sell, make money, and be left alone.

Try to imagine managing or working with these two Baby Boomers. It may be easy to generalize, making the mistake of saying they are alike because of their generation but that would not end well and is unfair to both individuals. Again, this is exactly why looking beyond generational perceptions is so important.

Finally, let's compare two Gen Xers, the age group that covers people ages 37 to 51 years old.

Gen Xer, Age 45	Gen Xer, Age 49
Managing partner	Principal consultant
20 direct reports	No direct reports
Married at age 24	Married at age 34
2 children (ages 14, 16)	1 child (age 2)
About to spend for college	Saving for college
"Empty nester" status is only a few years away	Elementary school is only a few years away
Started the company	Loyal to the company
Adapted to technology	Adapted to technology
Needs to work 10+ more years	Needs to work 20+ more years
Works on vacation	Unplugs completely on vacation

We saved this generational group for last, as your authors both represent Generation X. Beyond that label, as individuals, we require a deeper look. Though they are relatively close in age, one has 16- and 14-year-old daughters, and the other has a two-year-old daughter. One was competing in triathlons during his 30s and traveling, while the other was changing diapers and saving for college. This further substantiates why it is so important to look deeper in all cases, and it applies to Gen X as it does to each of the generations.

Within sales, generational diversity plays an interesting role. Not only does this topic impact an organization internally but, just as important, is the impact it causes between seller and buyer. Whether you are an employee learning how best to manage a relationship with a peer or boss, or you are a seller engaging buyers from multiple generations, let's begin to look at how our actions must be adjusted given what we now know.

· ·

Generational Flexibility:
Knowledge Is Important, Behavior Matters More

We are not experts on human behavior. Rather we are sales, sales leadership, and sales effectiveness experts—all of which happen to involve interpersonal communication and relationships. The TRACOM Group, which pioneered a model for assessing social style, define behavior as "What you say (verbal) and what you do (non-verbal)."[8] Generational behavior is quite similar. Over time people will reveal their generational tendencies through what they say and what they do. Our job is to use what we call Generational Flexibility to observe behavior and then decide to what degree, if at all, we need to adjust our approach.

Generational Flexibility is extremely valuable because it allows individuals to first understand the characteristics of generations, observe the behaviors of what people say and do in the workplace, and then adjust their approach in a manner that not only reduces tension, but leverages the individual's unique strengths in a way that benefits the individual and those around him or her. Our experience and research shows that individuals and teams that demonstrate high levels of Generational Flexibility increase their ability to communicate internally and sell their ideas across generational divides.

We have presented the concept of Generational Flexibility to Healthgrades, which hosts an online healthcare portal; through their platform, consumers can see information and ratings about a variety of healthcare providers. As a business, Healthgrades is an advertising firm that serves pharmaceutical companies and a variety of other healthcare-related advertisers. Mike Rosenberg, VP of sales, told us in an interview how flexible they have become as an organization given the advertising agencies they serve. Healthgrades employs a strong Gen X and Millennial sales team and the environment they have created allows the team to flourish. Mike told us that they embrace a casual setting, collaborate on team projects, and instill an environment in which open dialogue and new ideas are shared both internally and externally with customers. They drive for strong results but are highly aware of how people with different mindsets frame success. They have a strong culture of development, career pathing, coaching, and team selling. Sellers are challenged and leadership has adjusted well to the composition of their team.

When we spoke to Mike he cited his daily dress code as an example of Generational Flexibility. "I am sitting here today in jeans, a t-shirt, and a hoodie. Am I comfortable? No!" Mike was fairly open with the fact that he thought his outfit stretched the limits of business casual and is a far departure from the suits and ties that used to fill his closet. So why was Mike wearing an outfit he felt was borderline inappropriate? Recognizing the impact that a more laid-back dress code had on his direct reports allowed Mike to see past the traditions imprinted on him from prior generations. His team was relaxed, exponentially more productive, and appreciative of the simple concession Mike had made. Mike was exercising generational flexibility.

. . . .

Evaluating Common Generational Myths [9]

Generational myths and theories are shaped by clustering people, behavior, life-shaping events, access to technology, and stories told over time. Often the myths are carried on, exaggerated, and yet often end up representing an entire cluster of people. So often we hear the advice that organizations with a high percentage of Millennial employees should make the culture as "fun" as possible. But, when we asked sellers in our generational selling survey to score the importance of various manager qualities, all three generations scored the "creates a fun work environment" last, behind things like is "well-respected" or "gives me autonomy." You can see in the chart, as well, that Gen X sellers actually scored "creates a fun work environment" as more important than Millennials did!

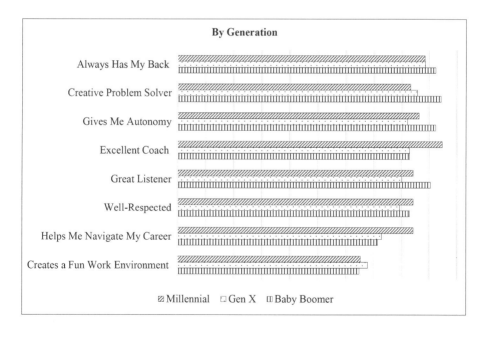

As we explore these myths, you will easily be able to think of people who may partly live up to them and others who are clearly the myth-busters. Let's consider a couple myths for each generation.

"Millennials are job hoppers."

Many people complain that Millennials will have five or more jobs before they hit their 30s. It's easy to blame "job hoppers" for high turnover costs, but businesses should consider what they aren't doing before assuming entitlement as the motivation for the departure. The reality is that Millennials are lifelong learners. They want to know everything about the work they do, the industry they are in, and how they fit into the big picture. Yes, many Millennials will change roles, but the days of having one job for decades isn't the standard for any generation. According to a survey conducted by Deloitte Consulting, only 37 percent of Gen Xers said they plan on staying with their current employers once the economy improves, compared to 44 percent of Gen Y and 52 percent of Baby Boomers.[10]

Myth confirmed: There are other factors to consider here than just a need to switch jobs every nine to 12 months. The transient nature of today's workforce could be due to the desire to grow professionally in an environment that simply remains challenging.

"Millennials don't work hard."

Working hard is a subjective term. If you are a Baby Boomer you may define working hard as 60 hours a week in the office. The Millennial may get the same amount of work, or more, completed in 40 hours and be unmotivated by being in the office all the time. Part of this is driven by perceptions, as a recent study from Bentley University shows "almost nine in 10 Millennials (89 percent) say they have a strong work ethic. But only 74 percent of non-Millennials believe they have as good a work ethic as that of older generations."[11] As opposed to work ethic and productivity, this myth seems to be grounded in the different priorities and expectations of the generational groups. As Leigh Buchanan, editor-at-large at *Inc.*

magazine, says, "One of the characteristics of Millennials, besides the fact that they are masters of digital communication, is that they are primed to do well by doing good. Almost 70 percent say that giving back and being civically engaged are their highest priorities."[12]

Myth busted: It depends on your perspective.

"Gen Xers are too cynical."

Pragmatic is a better description. This is all in the ear of the listener. Baby Boomers enjoy a healthy tone of pessimism and trust no one under their own age and Millennials are bubbling over with optimism. So what is left? Sounding cynical and jaded. However, each generation has experienced comparable levels of dissatisfaction, whether driven by economic recession, war, or political discord. Two Stanford sociologists have looked at cynicism across all generations and found "whatever the causes of disaffection, they are not ones that we Generation Xers experience uniquely, although we may very well feel our experience is unique."[13]

Myth busted: It is realism, not cynicism. Gen X just seems to "shoot the truth," and Baby Boomers would rather have it sugar coated in political correctness. Millennials hear reality as negativity. Gen X is just bad at inner thoughts.

"Gen Xers are slackers at work."

What is the definition of a slacker? "A person who avoids work and responsibilities," according to the dictionary.[14] This myth is likely brought to us by the Baby Boomer generation, the proud inventors of the 60-hour work week. Often Gen Xers are referred to as "slackers" when they do not work 10+ hour days—by Baby Boomers. Tom Gagnon, a high performing seller at Healthgrades, based in New York City, told us that when it comes to Gen X traits, he often hears that Gen X is lazy, but that is not something he has personally experienced. The reality is that Gen X employees travel (for work) and juggle family responsibilities in addition to managing work obligations, which was confirmed by a Pew Research survey that found Gen Xers trailing only Baby Boomers (but ahead of the Silent generation and Millennials) in work ethic.[15]

Myth busted: It's all about context, and others must consider the many responsibilities of Gen X, not just work.

"Baby Boomers are technology challenged."

We have yet to see any Baby Boomers walking around with stone tablets or drawing on cave walls. The world we in live allows virtually no human the chance to retreat from technology completely.

Myth busted: Yes, some Baby Boomers only use the smartphone for phone calls and not as their main lifeline. We travel often and observe Baby Boomers sporting all of the following: iPads, iPhones, smart watches, activity trackers, PCs, and every other popular gizmo. It seems that the dramatic improvements in the user interface of technologies pioneered by Apple have resulted in more technology literacy across the oldest and youngest generations. Research by digital marketing agency DMN3 "showed that an overwhelming 82.3 percent of Boomers belong to at least one social networking site."[16] It's time to move on.

"Baby Boomers are the original 'me' generation."

Given that many Baby Boomers came of age during the great post–WWII era of economic expansion and ushered in significant cultural changes, many have labeled this generation as selfish and "me first." Perhaps this was true when Baby Boomers were teenagers, but given that their roles have shifted, requiring an investment of both time and money to care for aging parents, "the so-called 'Me Generation' should really be considered the 'We Generation,'" according to Marc Freedman[17]

Myth busted: In the next 20 years, Baby Boomers are estimated to be donating more than $8 trillion in time and money.[18]

A Final Focus on Millennials

Two myths unique to Millennials require special focus. Through our work with our clients, we have seen the impact of these myths, and it is important that we bust these myths in order to begin moving forward in the right ways.

"Millennials expect everything to be handed to them."

In 2013, *Time* published a cover story titled "The Me Me Me Generation—Millennials Are Lazy, Entitled Narcissists Who Still Live With Their Parents,"[19] which seems to capture this brand or myth commonly attributed to Millennials, at least by older generations. In the workplace, there is a perception that entry-level Millennials want immediate promotions, but we believe this is just a misunderstanding among generations. As we described earlier, this is a generation that following the "Great Recession" of 2008–2010 has less income, more debt, lower mobility, and greater financial dependence on their parents than any other generation.

Myth busted: Millennials, just like other generations, want promotions, financial security, solid benefits, good leaders, aggressive performance-based compensation plans, and the chance for bonuses. That makes them no different than any other generation. The rub happens when they consistently ask older leadership for these things too often. Senior leaders hear this as being too eager and not displaying the same level of patience they demonstrated early in their careers. Unfortunately, business moves at near lightning speed today and the loyalty that individuals show for their organization is nowhere near where it used to be. Here is an example of a common interaction:

Millennial: Can we talk about what is next for me and how I can grow faster?

Senior leader, unspoken but thinking: Are you kidding me? I worked here for 18 years before I started to advance. This is unbelievable.

Some Millennials may have big aspirations with limited plans to actually make them come true. There is a correlation between this issue and being raised by parents who may have always told them that they could do anything they set their mind to. Leaders often perpetuate this belief encouraging a "speak your mind' culture, and then they are frustrated when Millennials do just that: speak their minds. The best advice we can present is for leaders to embrace the enthusiasm and look for ways to set forth realistic goals that drive performance.

"Millennials want to work for companies where they feel they are aligned with great purpose and support the mission of the organization."

We recently learned from one sales leader at a global technology company that his entry-level sales reps have a large financial burden due to college loans, expensive city rent, and rising healthcare costs. Due to their economic situation, there is a need for real earning potential. These forces are much more compelling than belief in a company's purpose and making the world a better place.

Myth busted: Consider the math for a Millennial entering a sales role at the age of 25 with a master's degree. They are burdened by significant student loan payments on top of paying rent for the first time. Add in other life expenses associated with getting to work, staying healthy, and salvaging something of a personal life, and they are likely eating ramen noodles for the foreseeable future. We see this all the time across industries and rarely hear that Millennials are quitting because they want to save the world. We work with a wide variety of clients with Millennials in sales roles and this motivation of "purpose" rarely comes up outside of a strong desire to create success for the customer and their team.

Rise Above Generational Stereotypes

By now you should understand the characteristics of each generation and the negative impacts associated with making assumptions based on sweeping stereotypes. We will now be shifting our focus on the ways in which individuals can adapt to meet the needs of each generation through the practice of Generational Flexibility. In order to be flexible, you have to be anticipatory, observant, and willing to adapt. Follow these three steps to avoid missteps and to set your organization on the right path.

Step 1: Be Aware

Armed with the right information to identify generational characteristics, it is important to remain aware that a single generation may not embody an individual entirely. Try to resist becoming susceptible to stereotyping that continues to perpetuate the generational divide. When meeting a new colleague, boss, or potential client for the first time, it will be difficult to know exactly how they prefer to be engaged. Remember the concepts of Generational Flexibility and begin to strategically navigate the interaction. This may include a change in the level of formality in your tone, physical demeanor, or even dress. Conversations will be a balancing act as sellers seek to minimize skepticism by proving a level of credibility all while trying not to sound completely self-absorbed and arrogant. These tips and tricks allow sellers to adjust to the individual being engaged.

Imagine you are about to have your eyesight examined. You are sitting about six feet away from a chart with letters constructed in an upside-down pyramid. The letters at the top are large and become smaller as the pyramid narrows toward the bottom of the chart. You read each row, starting at the top with the largest letters, and after each row the ophthalmologist adjusts the funny-looking lenses in an attempt to zero in on an eyesight diagnosis. The first engagement you have with a colleague or prospective client will unfold in the same methodical way. Start with the big-ticket, hot-button items, and begin to narrow the focus as you try to prescribe the best engagement approach for the individual in front of you.

Step 2: Observe Behavior

Observing behavior is a key tool for Generational Flexibility but also for effective interpersonal communications. Picking up on key indicators ensures that individuals are not pigeonholed into large generational buckets. Begin by observing their behavior in areas such as the types of questions they ask and how they communicate. Use what you can to determine as much as you can about the individual.

Beyond the first interaction, which is often the hardest part, observing behavior over time is critical. Observe people in action, talk to them, listen closely, and find out how people are wired. Ask yourself, "Am I thinking about one person or the majority of the team?"

Step 3: Adjust

Once you have digested the facts and observed behavior, it's time to adjust—or not. This step can be done at an individual level or for the masses. Based on your own tendencies, this may be a minor or major adjustment. It can mean adjusting how you prepare for a call or meeting, how you facilitate your next engagement, reviewing your guest list for an upcoming meeting, or tweaking the materials you plan to present. Awareness is only half the battle; putting this knowledge into practice is what separates you from others in your generational cohort.

Generational fluency and flexibility is achievable and now *you* have a roadmap to forge ahead. By being aware, observing behavior and making adjustments, individuals have the ability to navigate complex interactions, both internally and externally.

In the next chapter, we will move from knowledge to practice by illustrating the impact this topic has externally between buyer and seller. We will provide a perspective for how generational differences manifest themselves through customer interactions in order to help prevent issues or neutralize ones that may flare up during the sales process.

3

Changing Customer Interactions

"Every generation needs a new revolution."
—Thomas Jefferson, third president of the United States
(1743–1826)

A common practice for Symmetrics Group is to "shadow" our clients during sales meetings. As a silent observer of both internal meetings and sales calls, we have the unique ability to diagnose areas of inefficiency prior to tailoring a plan to overcome the identified issues. One such sales call involved a seller meeting with a large advertising agency based in Los Angeles. Our client requested that we shadow the seller assigned to the account. Prior to the call, David learned that the agency had recently made some staff changes and had requested a "lunch and learn" meeting. The agency lead was looking to educate the sales staff, creative team, and account reps on why and how to maximize direct mail media buys as part of a client's advertising mix.

The expectation was that the meeting was to be educational and engaging versus a traditional "pitch." The day of the session arrived and the

54-year-old Baby Boomer sales rep, with more than 20 years of experience, walked into the conference room to find 15 prospective buyers, all of whom were in their mid-to-late 20s, wearing skinny jeans and sporting non-traditional haircuts. From David's perspective, the vibe made it feel like an interesting place to work. As David looked across the room, he realized the sales rep was awkwardly and rather formally standing at the front of the room looking a bit shell-shocked in his three-piece suit. He came "prepared" for the meeting with a PowerPoint presentation, printed books, and sample advertising pieces as a leave-behind.

If it wasn't evident by the setting we just depicted, advertising agencies tend to employ a younger and hipper generation. These firms hire a large percentage of Millennials and assign them to manage sizable advertising accounts associated with high-profile clients. To be successful, sellers must often educate relatively inexperienced buyers who have influence over massive advertising budgets. The unprepared sales rep began pointing to the screen as he read his bulleted meeting agenda. After a few minutes, the mood of the meeting became uncomfortable. The audience was beginning to check out, lounging back in their chairs, and iPhones began to buzz. It was clear: the audience was bored and seemed slightly offended that they were being subjected to such a non-engaging and non-informative session. In what seemed like a hail Mary, one participant asked a question: "Can you give us an example of a client success story and how they targeted a specific segment of the market via direct mail? I'd like to see how the program worked for them." Instead of observing behavior and adjusting, the seller's response was robotic: "I would need to know more before I could show you a sample that specific. We have decades of experience targeting specific audiences and behaviors that we could share." Game over.

The sales rep was not adequately prepared to meet the client's objectives for this meeting, nor did he take the time to anticipate the needs of his audience. Without the right level of preparation, it's human nature to fall into a routine that is comfortable. What's more is that he didn't have the awareness to expand on their ideas or flex when a question was posed.

This Millennial audience of buyers was sensitive to how their actions will ultimately be perceived by their clients. They need to bring valuable insights to the table and prove that their recommendations are vetted and will prove impactful. They seek feedback from peers and mentors to ensure the decisions they make are sound and their recommendations unassailable. Had the seller anticipated that the Millennial buyers might want to learn how others in the industry had fared, or the general perception of direct mail in today's market, the seller could have engaged the audience by providing case studies, references, or a simple answer to the clearly articulated question. Instead he made a classic mistake by presuming that what had worked decades ago would still be applicable today.

The meeting ended badly and the agency lead was less than thrilled, especially because she told the sales rep to make sure the meeting was interactive, informative, and fun for the meeting participants. She even shared that the group had real concerns about the relevance of direct mail as a medium and that they wanted to ensure that what they were presenting to their clients was relevant and of value. The sales rep did not take her advice and missed an opportunity to engage an audience poised to heed the advice of an experienced and knowledgeable industry professional.

As more Millennials move into buying roles, evolving demographics in the workplace will continue to present both challenges and opportunities. In this chapter, we expand upon the generational differences defined previously and look at how they influence customer interactions. Nowhere are these changes more evident than in the sales process.

· ·

Silent Killers of Sales Progress

Today, sales professionals have the opportunity to leverage a variety of mediums to perpetuate their own personal brand and that of their company. Presentations no longer require an overhead projector and often demand a collaborative environment that is engaging and informative. Communication methods are no longer limited to a fax machine, phone call, or even a face-to-face meeting. With the advent of email and services like Skype and GoToMeeting, buyers have options. These options tend to lead to unique preferences and expectations. Setting up a Skype meeting with a Baby Boomer, looking for a little face time, is just one example of how these unpredictable preferences have the potential to silently kill your sales process before it even begins.

We consider generational differences that negatively impact customer interactions as "silent killers" of the sales process—because the differences are not typically vocalized. Can you imagine a world where people actually voiced their generational observations? Here are just a few examples of things we have actually heard when talking to customers of our clients:

- "Seriously, I have socks older than her."

- "I know I am moving fast with this demo; just try and keep up."

- "This guy has been around since the 1960s."

- "When the ink is dry on your degree, you will understand what I am talking about."

- "Why did we have to get together face to face?"

- "I can't trust someone younger than my own child."

- "I might buy from you, but I will never see you again because you won't be in this job more than three months."

- "These older sales reps are so slow to understand what we are dealing with, and I have no interest in going to lunch with them."

These inner thoughts are perfect examples for why sales professionals must evolve their approach to head off stereotyping and seek to provide immediate value when interacting with buyers.

A lot has changed, and generation-based preferences continue to have a direct impact upon sellers and their ability to successfully connect with buyers. When we asked survey participants about generational differences causing friction in the sales process, 66 percent of them said that generational differences "sometimes," "often," or "always" cause friction in the sales process.

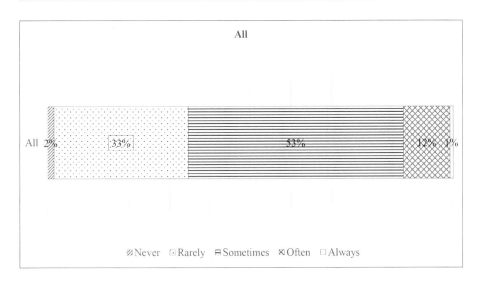

More interestingly, a higher percentage of Millennials, 84 percent, said that generational differences "sometimes" or "often" cause friction within their sales process, compared to 64 percent of Gen X and only 56 percent of Baby Boomers.

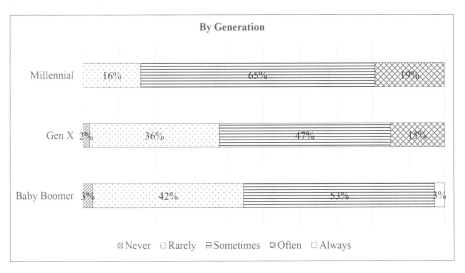

Millennials have been filling sales-related roles for more than a decade. In the last five years, however, we have seen a shift as Millennials are being provided with more decision-making authority. This new breed of buyer is requiring that all sellers, regardless of generation, remain adaptable and ready to meet the needs of their buyer.

Sellers should strategically map out certain tendencies and preferred styles of engagement. These generational hypotheses will need to be tested and tweaked but serve as a starting point, allowing missteps to be minimized to the best of their ability. Remember, though, that there are variables that may make this exercise challenging. By taking safe and calculated steps, sellers can become more aware of their approach and be ready to flex to the buyer when necessary.

Digging deeper into how generational diversity impacts the sales process, we asked survey participants to identify what actually causes generational friction in the sales process. Participants, regardless of generation or position, cited "communication style or method" as the number-one reason:

- 78 percent of executives say that "communication style or method" is the cause.

- 92 percent of managers say that "communication style or method" is the cause.

- 76 percent of sellers say that "communication style or method" is the cause.

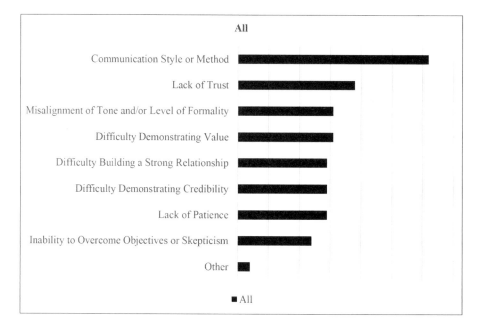

The good news is that "communication style or method" is completely coachable, as opposed to other, more difficult hurdles a seller might need to overcome like "lack of trust" or "difficulty demonstrating value." One recommended technique is to create a customer profile. Start by trying to identify the buyer's generation. Determine how you *think* they might want to be engaged, how formal of an approach will you take, and what information might be most important to them based upon where they are in the sales cycle. From there, try to determine how long they have been with the company, industry experience, length of time in their current role, level of influence, buying authority, and so forth. Define their professional network. Who do they work for? Who are their peers?

The goal of implementing Generational Flexibility is to learn how to minimize the impact of generational differences during customer interactions. Making these adjustments provides sellers with an opportunity to not only perpetuate the sales process but to expedite it!

· ·

Sales Process and the Customer Interaction

Virtually all B2B (business-to-business) sales organizations have some form of a sales process that is taught, universally understood, coached to, and likely implemented within a CRM (customer relationship management) system in support of pipeline management and forecasting requirements. To better understand changing customer interactions, we must have a baseline understanding of what "best practice" means relative to a specific sales processes methodology. Think of the following definitions as a broad way to understand a typical B2B sales process. Remember: both the buyer and the seller have a unique set of goals. Though the following steps represent seller expectations, these steps are often aligned to the client's buying cycle.

Sales Process Stages

- **Stage 1: Identify.** Seller identifies suspects, engages in early attempts to secure a meeting with the buyer(s), and begins to qualify a potential opportunity.

- **Stage 2: Discover.** Seller engages with initial buyer(s) and conducts initial conversations/meetings. Both parties share information, and the seller continues to qualify based on fit with the buyer's needs and requirements.

- **Stage 3: Develop.** Seller validates fit with the buyer's needs and requirements, engages with multiple buyers and influencers to create the initial scope and investment for a potential solution. Both seller and buyer typically align around common milestones and a time line to complete the buying/sales process.

- **Stage 4: Compete.** Seller determines the final scope and investment, positions their solution against the known competitors, and manages potential obstacles and objections as they seek verbal agreement from the buyer.

- **Stage 5: Close.** Seller completes the final negotiations and signs agreement with the buyer.

Generational differences impact the sales process in a number of ways. Let's look at Stage 1: Identify. Over time, the Identify stage has changed dramatically. The days of phone books, lead lists, cold-calling, and door-knocking have evolved into the world of LinkedIn, Google, social media and other forms of "warmer" lead development. Millennials seem to thrive in this world, Gen X has found ways to adapt, and Baby Boomers are trying to unlock the real potential behind their network. Pew Research has found that whereas 88 percent of Millennials in the United States own a smartphone, only 46 percent of "older Boomers" (ages 60–69) do.[1] However, the reality is not as it seems and especially not what's been perpetuated in almost every article on the topic on generational diversity in the workplace. Sales organizations must not assume that all Millennials are adept at identifying and targeting the right prospects. They may know how to use the platform but for very different purposes. When it comes to getting that first meeting, the generation falls short of expectations for two reasons: They often don't have the business acumen to decipher the right point of content, and the level of formality is often so low it can often resonate as offensive to the buyer.

In the same way that Millennials are identified as naturally "tech savvy," Boomers are labeled the opposite. Boomers may not be as familiar with the medium, but the network that resides in their rolodex is rich with the right prospects, given their tenure and experience as sellers. This conundrum is a perfect example (to be explored in Chapter 4), which requires organizations to not only equip sellers with the tools but the training to overcome their generational stereotypes in order to navigate this new prospecting environment.

One of our client's sales processes illustrates a similar challenge. This company provides high-tech IT outsourcing and data center services with sales teams that are divided between large market and mid-market level accounts. The mid-market sellers spend a majority of their time prospecting, as they do not have a large base of existing high-revenue customers. The leader of this team, a Baby Boomer, shared some frustrations with a group of sellers—in this case, Millennials. The problem is one of context and experience.

The sellers primarily work their territories to develop new client relationships by building a strong voice on LinkedIn, connecting on professional platforms, and reaching out through email and marketing campaigns. The problem isn't that sellers are unable to provide meaningful and relevant content within the social space or even that they aren't targeting the right prospects. Turns out they are excellent at perpetuating the company's brand and curating a personal voice that increases their own credibility. Unfortunately, the sales leader continues to feel frustrated because the sellers are not generating enough "top of the funnel" activity, like face-to-face sales calls and in-person visits. They are taking too long, and wasting too much time, trying to get a viable level of sales activity established.

The sellers take a very passive approach to their prospecting efforts, but in all fairness, they never learned a different approach for engaging prospects and landing an initial meeting. To these Millennial sellers, the idea of picking up a phone and calling a cold prospect sounds foreign. The sales leader has enough experience to know that at some point, if you're not closing any business, you must use a more direct approach in order to start a dialogue. Put yourself in the role of this sales leader. How would you handle this situation?

In our view, the solution is somewhere in the middle. We cannot ignore the tools we have today, nor can we just "smile and dial," but sales leaders must set clear expectations for what "Identify" in the sales process really entails. In this example, after a bit of coaching, the sales leader now works much more closely with the Millennial sales reps to help them determine when they have completed enough "brand building." The leader has invested the time and effort into teaching these sellers how to engage and earn face-to-face sales calls.

Impact of the Generations on Buying Behavior

Changing demographics mean that it's not just younger sellers selling to older buyers anymore. In fact, there are now a variety of generations represented by buyers. Our own research shows that 50 percent of buyers are from Gen X, 34 percent of buyers are Baby Boomers, and 18 percent of buyers are Millennials.[2] We also explored how much sellers from a particular generation were selling to buyers of another generation. The data revealed that Millennial sellers are selling to a higher percentage of Millennial buyers (23 percent), but still there is a strong mix of generations in both seller and buyer roles.

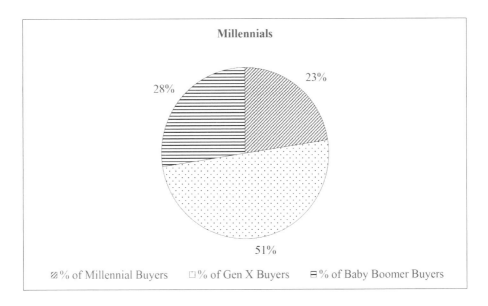

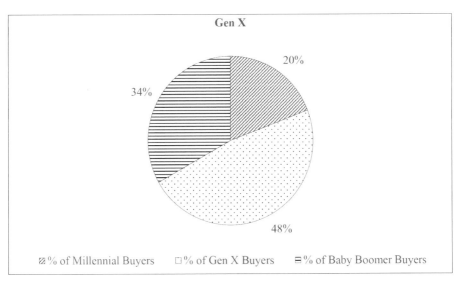

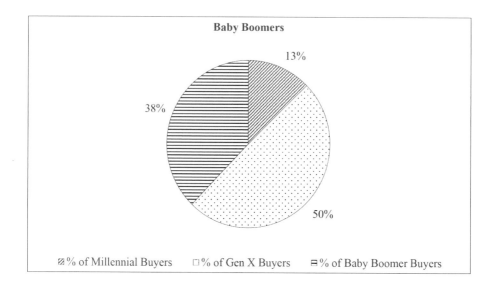

In our line of work, we have seen buyers represented by each generation. We have observed how they behave differently in meetings and during sales pursuits. Based on our observations, we have developed several tips for sellers selling to buyers from a generation other than their own, which typically cover one or more steps in the sales process.

The Millennial Buyer

- When prospecting Millennial buyers, do not forget about social media channels. More and more buyers find out about a new product or service offering on websites like LinkedIn, Twitter, Instagram, and Snapchat. Sellers should not hesitate to leverage their social networks to generate leads, source references, or build their credibility via personal brand management.

- You can't assume that they lack knowledge of your offering and that of your top three competitors. With instant access to the web, this techno-savvy buyer is doing the majority of their research before they even make their needs known.

- Be wary of inflated roles or titles, and remember that the matrixed organizational structure, and therefore a matrixed decision-making process, is becoming more and more prevalent. Try to identify who else will be influencing their decision and make content relevant and easy to share so that they can get feedback from their network.

- Put some thought into a multimedia presentation and the various modes of communication. It is important to give Millennial buyers the perception that sellers are up to speed with the newest trends in technology, and therefore will be easy to work with.

- Demonstrate responsiveness. Remember that Millennials grew up with information at their fingertips, and in the buying process, they will demand information just as quickly. In the same regard, know that once they make a decision, they will want to move fast, so sellers should be sure to have everything in place to help their buyers get started with the new product or service quickly.

The Gen X Buyer

- Leverage technology. Gen X buyers have had all the gizmos and presentation options in their world for a couple decades now. Sellers should also aim to provide appropriate materials before the meeting to fulfill their need to "get to the point" in meetings.

- Be prepared for the Gen X buyer to be a little skeptical. This is a result of being involved in several economic downturns and corporate disappointments. Present the true substance of what you can offer and how that ties to upside for them and their business.

- Don't be thrown off by cutting or edgy speak. Gen X buyers will probably speak exactly what is on their mind, so sellers must resist the temptation to take it personally or get too spirited in debates that could turn the meeting downright hostile.

- Bring new or innovative solutions to the table. Remember that Gen X has seen the world turned upside down via economic crisis, and at this point in their career, they are likely to be willing to take risks and break rules if there is a compelling reason.

- Be respectful of your Gen X buyer's time. They do not want things to take longer than they have to and your ability to keep up will help you engender loyalty.

The Baby Boomer Buyer

- Make every effort to meet with your Baby Boomer buyer in person. Many Baby Boomers will need to feel like they are comfortable with the seller before they can ever get comfortable with the product or solution. Avoid multi-tasking or trying to explain too many things at once. Turn off your phone, turn off instant message, and make sure there is a laser focused on your buyer and the task at hand.

- Consider ways to make sales presentation as "high touch" as possible. Have Baby Boomer buyers demo your product or service, or invite your CEO or president to your final sales pitch. Extra touches like this will go further with your Baby Boomer buyers.

- Build trust among your Baby Boomer buyers. This goes beyond having a good in-person rapport. Consider avenues like a great reference, past case study of success, or even just demonstrating that you understand their business really well.

- Demonstrate a strong work ethic. Don't be afraid to leverage after-work hours to have dinner with the buyer and his or her team. Showing an effort to go the extra mile will demonstrate the persistence and patience you need to earn their business.

• • • • • • •

Understanding the ways that generational nuances influence buyer behaviors is one way to keep the sales process on course and moving in the right direction. Theresa, a Millennial account manager at Houzz, sells digital advertising to mom-and-pop interior designers and contractor businesses. Her older clients, like many in the industry, are unwilling to spend money on digital advertising. To them "advertising" means post cards, magazines or tangible, hard-copy collateral that designers or contractors can use to display their work. Her clients' aversion to "digital" media seems to also cause issues during her sales process, as many clients struggle to follow along in virtual sales meeting environments. Web-based conference meetings are extremely painful and some have challenges even opening email attachments. Technology is not, nor has it ever been, an integral part of doing business for Theresa's clientele.

For sales organizations targeting companies like these, it can be difficult to balance the client's needs (tangible, face-to-face interaction) while utilizing technology as a way to reduce costs and achieve economies of scale. Understanding their target market, Houzz has recently equipped their sellers with a special virtual presentation program called ClearSlide[3], which, in Theresa's view, is a more simplistic virtual presentation tool designed for buyers that are less comfortable with technology. Theresa has her own personal link that her buyers can type in, which she finds much easier than other web-conferencing tools that require multiple passcodes, program downloads, or plug-ins that cause technological difficulties. Though not all Baby Boomer buyers struggle with technology, it's important that companies understand their audience. By making sellers aware of what is to be expected, and arming them with communication tools better suited to their target market, companies have the ability to close the gap between the buyer and seller. Investing in a communication tool that will better target the generation of the buyer is just one example. Another might be tapping an internal subject matter expert to include in an upcoming sales call. A Boomer selling to a Millennial buyer may decide to include a Millennial colleague the same way a Millennial selling to a Boomer buyer may do the reverse. Coming to the table with a subject matter expert can not only illustrate bench strength but subtly communicates that "We get you!"

. . . .

Interaction From the Customer's Perspective

By utilizing the tips outlined in the prior section, sellers have an ability to overcome the silent killers of the sales process. Let's now shift gears and take a look at how it feels to be the buyer.

From our clients and their customers, we repeatedly hear stories that paint the picture of a changing customer interaction. Following are a sampling of direct quotes and stories from recent engagements. See if you can identify where possible generational clashes could affect the buyer-seller interaction.

Value of In-Person Interactions

Client: I can't do business with certain types of suppliers. I disqualify them right away.

Symmetrics Group: What types of suppliers are you referring to?

Client: Well, I have a fair number of suppliers who only call me, email me, and never even think of taking the time to come in here and establish a relationship. I can hear the boiler room of sellers in the background when they call, and if you do not have the integrity to come in here, learn about our business, and gain my trust, I can't do business with you. Even if your prices are substantially lower than what I am paying, trust beats 'fly by night' behavior every time.

Which generations are clashing? This is a Baby Boomer procurement buyer making decisions about suppliers based upon his generational trust requirements. She will not bend her preferences and the sellers calling on her are deploying the tools and methods they are told to use in order to build a book of business: phones and computers. The buyer is demanding that the seller adapts, yet the seller feels unable to meet the needs of this large prospect based on limitations in how he is allowed to engage the prospect. The customer ended up following through with a risky and expensive implementation that his current supplier steered him through based on earning trust and providing significant face time. New sellers, deploying modern techniques, have all failed in the pursuit of this client.

Bringing Insights to the Customer Conversation

Client statement: I am so busy that if a sales rep wants my time, they have to show me real, tangible value and get to the point. I can't waste time educating them on what we do and how we do it.

Symmetrics Group: How often does that happen today?

Client: Too often, in my opinion. I get sales reps from many different types of businesses who stroll in here with lists of questions about what we do and how we do it. That is what our website and research time are for. I understand open-ended questioning, but I can't waste an hour on it. If you have my time, I need you to understand us well enough to be able to carry a dialogue and provide some thought leadership."

This Gen X buyer is fed up with solution selling that encourages sales reps to "find the pain" instead of bringing ideas to the table. Interestingly, the seller was also Gen X and has been trying very hard to be overly consultative. This was not about earning face time; it was about over-engineering discovery when the buyer has limited time to focus. Sellers have access to research tools, a ton of information, and other ways to generate knowledge before a meeting. Additionally, in a world where companies do more with less people, prospects have less time to chat in meetings. That means that sellers must have the base knowledge to drive meaningful conversations and bring content that drives value. Too much relationship-building and chit-chat will not work anymore—especially with a Gen X buyer who has a need to get to the point, debate, and validate the competence of the seller.

Meeting With Customers

Client: I have a sales rep who called me and asked to hop a flight to New York City if he was able to land a meeting with a key buyer later that night.

Symmetrics Group: What?

Client: The seller lives in Chicago and is trying to unlock a deal with a key agency we work with. He is going to invite them to an evening spin class that they love and feels he can get face time with them in this setting. He called today and offered them the passes to the class and they accepted. He wants to fly right now to NY, take them to the class tonight, and then do a few drinks after to find out why the deal has not moved along. I said yes since this is a big deal and it seems to be the only way to get the face time we need.

This Millennial seller is trying to develop a solution for a team of Millennial buyers. Unable to get the face time he needs to validate the buyer's needs and requirements, the seller got creative. He knows that they tend to blend the boundaries between social and professional and that these Millennial buyers, in particular, are very health conscious. We heard this story and thought of ourselves as sellers. We can't think of many clients that would have responded the way this group ultimately responded. Many of our clients would have considered 60 minutes of spinning worse than a 60-minute sales pitch. Older generations often feel like fine wine and big steaks at a swanky restaurant is an absolutely appropriate approach for engaging with prospective clients they are looking to impress. Although these types of interactions have been mainstays for decades, they may not be the best option when it comes to swaying the hearts and minds of Millennial decision-makers. To Millennials, time is of the utmost importance. They would rather be offered a spot in a spin class or a lesson in cold-press coffee brewing instead of being "schmoozed" or "sold to," albeit at a fancy restaurant. Melding social experiences with work provides a multi-tasking environment in which these young decision-makers find utility and value in the experience. At the same time, sellers are provided with an opportunity for valuable face time.

• • • • • • •

Now that we have looked at a few examples of the changing customer interaction, let's look at how to neutralize possible generational differences.

Playing Offense and Not Defense

It is our opinion that a well-conceived offense prevents sellers from ever having to play defense. This approach helps sellers effectively implement their sales process across any generational divide. Though it is always important for sellers to evaluate the customer's behaviors, and adjust appropriately, sellers should focus on the following before, during, and after a sales meeting.

Before a Meeting

Sellers should prepare a meeting agenda and organize materials in a manner that aligns with what the client might anticipate. Sellers should also prepare fellow colleagues, who are to be included in the meeting, by clearly defining roles and responsibilities, crafting discovery topics/ questions, planning to bring insights and relevant ideas, and preparing a well-rounded presentation that addresses the "who, how, what, and why" in order to engage each decision-maker and/or influencer. Sellers should also plan for possible objections, prepare how they will adjust if the meeting gets cut short, think through the best possible outcomes, and plan to keep true to the customers' WIIFM (what's in it for me?).

Remember: to avoid a generational guessing game, sellers should research their buyer and create client profiles for each meeting participant to get a feel for backgrounds and roles. These can be confirmed during the meeting.

During the Meeting

Sellers should introduce the agenda early and gain feedback on what else the customer may want to address, stay on task, and be willing to adjust to the customers' demands. Manage the meeting agenda, present with confidence, and seek to understand the motivating factors associated with objections and areas of concern. Probe deeper before responding, clearly present your presentation, and take detailed notes making sure to clarify key actions required after the meeting. Action items should be assigned to either the seller or buyer, and expectations for follow-up are to be agreed upon by both parties.

Throughout the meeting, sellers have the distinct opportunity to observe the behavior of the buyer. Whether on the phone or face-to-face, a buyer will give clues that are easy to pinpoint on the generational continuum. Sellers should take every opportunity to confirm their suspicions as they relate to assumed generation-based preferences. For example, confirm that the meeting medium works for the client. It would be important to know whether or not the individual would have preferred a face-to-face meeting or, perhaps, is now comfortable taking future calls via web conference. Being sensitive and accommodating goes a long way as sellers seek to engender loyalty and build a better relationship with their buyer.

After the Meeting

Sellers should look for ways to share new insights or knowledge and remain "professionally persistent" without adding so much additional pressure that they turn people away. It will be important for sellers to remain top of mind. Sending a thank-you note (written or email), proactively following up on items the customer promised, and staying on top of deliverable due dates will allow Boomers to trust and verify. By providing references that aid decision-making, Millennial buyers will be able to easily poll their network, and by highlighting possible obstacles and objections a Gen Xer will feel more empowered to push the status quo. Remaining vigilant, by continuing to observe behavior, will serve sellers well and by adjusting the client profile, sellers can pinpoint how best to continue serving their buyers in a way that caters to the needs of the buyer.

• • • • • • •

These actions are 100 percent in the control of the seller. Regardless of any possible generational divide that may exist between the seller and the buyer, a seller who puts each of these items into common practice will avoid possible generational flare ups and become more adept at wielding Generational Flexibility. Sellers who play a strong sales execution offense will avoid having to play generational nuance defense.

Building Trust

One of the hallmarks of a successful business-to-business sale is the level of trust between the buyer and the seller. Certainly the level and need for personal trust varies based on the type of sale: low for a commodity purchase like some paper products and high for legal or management consulting services. Think of trust as happening on a slow clock; it's not instantly earned during the sales process unless a substantial relationship, business or personal, is already in place. Regardless of the product or service, people do not usually choose to do business with people they either do not get along with or don't trust. Charlie Green, the author of *Trust-Based Selling*, describes trust as an equation:

$$\text{Trust} = \text{Credibility} + \text{Reliability} + \text{Intimacy/Self-Orientation}$$

We are big fans of Charlie and his work, and have seen the application of this formula through both our clients' and our own selling experiences. But how do generational differences impact trust? Let's look at each variable in the equation in order to determine how generational nuances can cause obstacles while also providing opportunities.

As it relates to generational preconceived notions, **credibility** is tricky. When the buyer and seller are from the same generation, a level of comfort and camaraderie is felt within the interaction. Though we wouldn't say buyers and sellers from the same generation provide a level of instant credibility, it does help set the foundation. When buyer and seller are from different generations, there are a few scenarios to consider. For instance, Gen X sellers may appear at the right place in their careers to exude a certain level of credibility, whereas Millennials and Boomers must work harder to prove their credibility. Millennials are often labeled as less credible due to an assumed lack of experience. Boomers, on the other hand, have a great deal of experience but can be categorized as antiquated and unaware of the current problem set facing today's buyer.

Sellers must take steps to overcome these preconceived notions. Millennials must immediately demonstrate a profound understanding of the customer's problems, deliver immediate insights, and display a solid understanding of the product. Case studies can be leveraged to indicate a track record of the product's success, in lieu of personal experience, and curated references can help to credential even the shortest of resumes. All generations should leverage their experience where applicable and stay current with problems plaguing buyers. Remaining proficient with technology and communication mediums is also an easy way to remain on top of the game.

Reliability is a given when it comes to being a professional seller, irrespective of age. This is a constant in the trust equation and should be managed as such. **Intimacy**, however, has a large impact on the trust equation and is often the physical proof point that allows sellers to gauge how the relationship is progressing. Intimacy boils down to being well connected with the client. Consequently, the client equally values the relationship on both a professional and likely a personal level.

Think back over the past 12 to 24 months. Were certain relationships better than others? What was the level of intimacy you had with those buyers? Intimacy with your customers can often be measured through client evidence. Does the client answer your calls during, or after, business hours? Do you know what your client likes and values outside of the office? Are they candid and honest about things they do not like? Do they take reference calls? Have you done things socially together? Do you know about their kids, pets, or upcoming vacation plans? In each of these dialogues, are you focused on your needs or your customers? **Self-orientation** comes from having a primary focus on yourself and your goals versus those of your customer.

Each of these variables is critical when turning customer interactions into lasting relationships. Any relationship, personal or professional, requires trust. So, when defining a successful customer interaction, remember these four variables, as they are inextricably linked.

• • • • • • •

We have looked closely at the changing landscape associated with customer interactions, and how the ground beneath our feet continues to shift. Too much has changed to keep doing what has always been done, with no regard to how generational perceptions only seem to exacerbate the situation for sellers. In the next chapter, we will take a look at how sales organizations must address critical areas in order to support sellers attempting to navigate these complex customer interactions.

4
How Sales Organizations Must Adapt

"There was no respect for youth when I was young, and now that I am old, there is no respect for age—I missed it coming and going."

—J.B. Priestly, English novelist, playwright, social commentator, and broadcaster (1894–1984)

A few years ago, we observed a sales call for an IT outsourcing company that was presenting to an online "bridge funding" firm. This firm provides short-term capital to small businesses. The potential customer needed hosting capabilities in several global regions and had plans to open offices in several new countries. The sales meeting included the seller, her sales leader, and three buyers from the financing firm. Given who was sitting at the table, we quickly made several generational assumptions based on the apparent ages of the group: the sales rep was a Millennial, the sales leader was a Baby Boomer, and all three buyers were Millennials. The dialogue among the buyers was informal, rather direct in tone, and included some strong dislike for their current vendor. Having seen the materials for the meeting only an hour or so prior, we were concerned. They were carrying standard slides and a few basic ideas on how the solution might work based on history and preliminary research, but no thought leadership or relevant references. It became apparent, from the buyers' questions, that they were seeking more information on actual technical capabilities. They wanted best-in-class thinking, evidence of other solutions in a similar industry, and real answers to very specific questions based on their business objectives. The client was ready to get into the details and not hear the "pitch."

How does this represent ways that sales organizations must adapt? This situation, an extremely collaborative environment driven by Millennials on both sides of the table, called for a non-traditional sales approach. In an attempt to prove a level of credibility, the sellers came prepared with potential solutions based on the information they had already identified by researching the prospect and decision-makers. Unfortunately, the client did not want the typical "show and tell" that so many sales organizations seem to be very comfortable delivering. These Millennial buyers wanted to collaborate, challenge one another, and build a solution rooted in proven industry results. In the end, the IT outsourcing company adjusted by bringing in technical resources to create a more collaborative setting and leveraged case studies to prove its successful track record. The prospect could now start to shape a solution while using the technical resources to challenge their own thinking. How did the organization change? By getting more people in the collaborative process and limiting the "pitch."

This sales organization is an excellent example of a generationally flexible team that felt empowered to do what was required to meet the needs of their prospective client. This seemed like an obvious solution, right? The client wants to collaborate, so let's bring in the technical experts and have an open conversation about the potential needs of the prospect. Unfortunately, some organizations create artificial barriers that require all communications be routed through a single point of contact.

The mindfulness and subsequent shift in how the organization approached these types of problems did not come naturally. The IT outsourcing company had engaged our firm to initiate a full "Way of Sales" assessment. After acknowledging the need for a full sales transformation, the firm began digging in based on several prioritized areas identified within the assessment. As discovery with the client began, we identified the impact generational differences were having within several areas of their organization. The IT firm is now going to market more prepared for each sales call and the teams spend significantly more time analyzing how to maximize each interaction based on seller and buyer generational discrepancies. Sellers have been given tools to guide their practice, and sales leaders are engaging and coaching sellers in the field.

Although generational dynamics permeate all aspects of business operations, there are a few specific areas that we believe every organization can, and should, address. In this chapter, we cover our Way of Sales model and highlight how generational nuances affect each Way of Sales quadrant. This chapter also includes a simple assessment that helps organizations identify their biggest opportunities to adapt to generational differences in their workforce and in the field. In Chapters 5 through 7, we will drill down on specific impacts to areas such as recruiting and onboarding, sales skills development, performance management, and coaching.

· ·

Generational Considerations to the Way of Sales

At Symmetrics Group, we developed our Way of Sales model to help companies drive their overall sales objectives in a focused and disciplined manner, and this model has also proven extremely useful when exploring the impacts of generational diversity. Utilized to diagnose the need for wholesale sales transformations, these four focus areas can provide a framework for understanding how and where generational diversity impacts sales organizations. There are many levers a company can pull in order to achieve higher results. Although we are not recommending the need for a wholesale sales transformation, we do recognize the impact generational diversity has on certain areas more than others. Here we have outlined and defined each of the four categories,. In doing so, organizations can easily identify and prioritize strategic action plans for the topics that are impacting their business:

1. **Strategy and Structure:** Defines who you are selling to, what you are selling, how you are selling, and why you are different—all based on the desired returns for the sales organization (revenues – cost of sales).

2. **Processes and Tools:** Defines the sales processes and enabling tools to support execution of the sales strategy.

3. **Enablement and People:** Ensures effective and efficient execution of sales processes through recruiting, enabling, and retaining the best people with the right messages and skills.

4. **Metrics and Management:** Outlines the metrics, sales coaching, and sales management practices that materially impact sales results and the quality of sales execution.

Each one of these four areas has several sub-categories to consider. Let's look at some examples of how generational differences impact each category.

. . . .

Strategy and Structure

The principles behind the first area of Strategy and Structure help companies think holistically about how they should "go to market" to achieve their sales targets. By analyzing both the sales strategy and structure of their sales team(s), organizations can ensure an appropriate balance between sales effectiveness (hitting your sales goals) and sales efficiency (hitting your cost of sales targets/budget).

Sales Strategy

Who are your customers? How do they buy? How many sales people are needed and with what level of skill and experience? These are only a few examples of the types of questions sales and marketing executives must address when building and evaluating the strategy and structure of their sales organization. A key area of focus for sales and marketing leaders is how to assess their current and potential customers. Often companies divide customer markets into discrete segments based on characteristics such as industry vertical, revenue size, and geography. These segments typically have different needs, buying processes, and revenue implications. As we explore the effects of multiple generations on an organization's sales strategy and structure, the first place to begin is with the ideal customer.

Increasingly in some industries, such as advertising and technology, Millennials are moving into positions with "buying" authority. A recent report by the B2B marketing agency Sacunas found that "73 percent of Millennials are involved in product or service purchase decision-making at their companies. Approximately one-third of Millennials report being the sole decision-maker for their department."[1] Sacunas research also supports our findings that Millennials leverage digital sources (e.g., search engine, vendor websites, social media) and peer input more than advice from a sales professional when making a purchasing decision. We interviewed Eric Middleton, who is in a senior leadership role with a startup firm called Gladly, based in Silicon Valley. He has more than 20 years of experience including Oracle, PeopleSoft, and a handful of other very successful startups. At Gladly, Eric employs a balance of Millennial and Gen X sellers. He finds that his younger sellers are particularly attracted to the fast-paced startup environment, flat organizational structure, and the chance to be a part of something that has the potential for enormous growth and success. Eric told us, "When thinking about the sales cycle, younger people want to be in a high-transaction type of selling environment and are less interested in sales cycles that may last several years. Reason being, Millennial sellers are eager to use their recently acquired selling skills to learn what works and how to adjust." Unfortunately, not all sales cycles are the same. Depending on the company, and the product or service being offered, the sales process may be exponentially longer. Highly complex or consultative offerings will require due process and more time to consider any, and all, implications a decision may have on other areas of the business. Here's the rub: Millennials are wired for instant gratification and constant feedback. Everything they desire is a few clicks away. Imagine having to wait 12 to 18 months to determine if you are doing well in your endeavors and to determine if your hard work is paying off.

In order to cater to this need, Eric organized his team to take advantage of these motivating attributes. By aligning his Millennials sellers with the more transactional-level accounts, they are able to hone their skills. An added benefit for Eric is that these transactional accounts are considered the low-hanging fruit. Given revenues are lower for these transactional accounts, Eric's Millennial sellers can practice their craft in a less financially risky environment. You can also expect that the highly prized "white whales," constantly being prospected, will be less likely to respond to indirect and social selling scenarios. Fortunately for the Millennials, the smaller market niche Eric has created is responding well to these tactics.

On Gladly's large, strategic accounts, Eric has built a sales team comprised mainly of Gen X sales reps who focus on sales processes that are more traditional in terms of in-person meetings and tend to exhibit longer sales cycles. Eric's success lies in finding the right Millennials and aligning their motivations to fit perfectly with the job and how Gladly has decided to go to market. We spoke with one of Eric's Millennial sales reps, who told us that prior to Gladly, he worked at a very large U.S. bank in a business development role. He described the pace of sales there as long and painful, and the work environment as "sterile." Since joining Gladly, the Millennial seller has thrived, given the fast-paced, entrepreneurial environment and the opportunity to leverage technology as a prospecting tool and in building his personal brand.

Sales Team Structure

Another important area within Strategy and Structure is an organization's ability of to balance effectiveness and efficiency (e.g., cost of sales) with blended teams and roles. A good example is leveraging an "inside" sales team to perform parts, or all, of the sales process given client size, complexity, and customer dispersion. It costs time and money to send sellers to see prospects and customers face-to-face and typically these resources are expensive. Companies often utilize inside sales teams for business development (prospecting), servicing smaller existing accounts, upselling value-added services to existing customers, appointment-setting for outside sales reps, and reactivating lost accounts. For most companies, maintaining a blend of inside and field-based sales teams allows them to balance the overall cost of sales with sales effectiveness, and match the comparative strengths of a multigenerational sales team to the way their customers purchase their products and services.

A Fortune 100 enterprise technology firm has recently launched a new sales team focused on combining digital marketing, social selling, and traditional inside sales methods to target changing buyers. In an interview, the leader of this team described the target buyers for this new sales capability this way:

> "The buyers are changing on both the consumer and B2B side. All of those buying behaviors from the consumer side (think Amazon and ecommerce sites) are creeping into the B2B world. We want to intersect with those people doing research online and become more relevant. If Millennials are doing 80 percent of the research prior to ever talking to someone, we need to get in front of them and become more top of mind with things like digital ads, keywords, banners—all to assist with the buyer's journey."

He indicated that their target customers are primarily Millennials and also those Gen Xers whose buying habits are changing like those of Millennials.

In addition to building a team of mostly Millennial talent to target fellow Millennial corporate IT buyers, this sales leader has focused on several other sales strategy elements including the use of "multi-channel digital advertising and networking campaigns to drive qualified sales leads to the team." By establishing a partnership model with value-add resellers (VARs) and independent software vendors (ISVs), and implementing multi-channel marketing strategies with those partners, many large technology companies are taking the necessary steps to set up new channels in order to target and communicate to a new generation of B2B buyer.

· ·

Processes and Tools

Based on how your customers buy your solutions, what are the major steps in the sales process? If you mention the word *process* to salespeople, you may get chased from the room. However, a well-designed, client-aligned sales process helps to define a predictable and repeatable path for sales success and serves as a framework for the supporting tools and technologies that help make the process more effective (i.e., win more business).

Sales Processes and Methodologies

In the United States, organizations spend approximate $2.5 billion[2] annually on sales training. There are many well-established programs that cover everything from one-call sales cycles to complex sales processes lasting between 12 and 24 months. Even with the advent of the popular "Challenger" sales training program based on the best-selling book *The Challenger Sale*,[3] many of the concepts and models are based on selling methods developed and popularized in the 1970s and 1980s, that are still relevant today. Increasingly, these methods and tools continue to be utilized and their relevance extended through the advent of social selling platforms. The most common example is LinkedIn. For a "hunter" sales professional charged with generating revenue within a strategic set of accounts, or territory, LinkedIn is an excellent resource for researching company contacts, decision-makers, and influencers who can help provide "warm" introductions. This tool also provides buyers with a way of evaluating potential vendors and partners. As Chris Dessi, CEO of Silverback

Social and CNN correspondent on social media, told us, "There is no reason a sales executive, in today's selling environment, should not have a fine tuned digital posture. What happens if your cold-calling and someone decides to Google you before reaching back out? If you haven't curated content that reinforces your credibility and begins building trust with your potential buyer, you are dead in the water."

In our survey, we asked participants about their use of social selling as part of their sales process. We defined social selling as "when sellers leverage social media platforms to perpetuate their personal and corporate brand in order to build credibility and engage directly with prospects and customers." We actually found that more survey respondents, 34 percent "never" or "rarely" use social selling as part of their sales process, compared to 27 percent who "often" or "always" do.

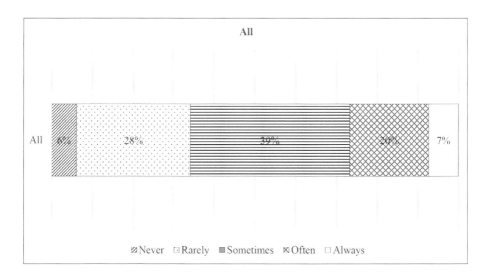

The use of social selling by the different generations surprised us as well: 36 percent of Baby Boomers said they "often" or "always" use social selling as part of their sales strategy, compared to only 26 percent of Millennials and 23 percent of Gen Xers.

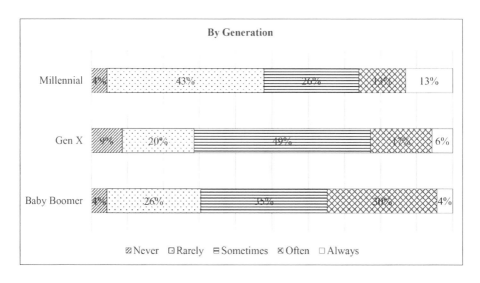

Even more surprising was the fact that nearly half of the Millennial responders said they "never" or "rarely" use social selling as part of their sales strategy. Our view is that, although many Millennials have grown up with technology and various social media outlets, they may not yet possess a network of potential prospects. Though their number of connections may eclipse that of a Gen Xer or Baby Boomer, many of these connections are peers and most are not yet in decision-making roles. Another point to consider is that having grown up with more personal social sites, such as Facebook, Millennials may avoid the platforms altogether so as not to perpetuate a stereotype. Organizations must recognize the internal struggle these stereotyped sellers are contending with. They must be encouraged and trained on how to curate relevant content, understanding with whom and when that content should be shared during the sales process. It's not enough to have 1,000+ connections. It's more important to understand how to leverage the network they have to connect with the network they want.

Companies have a huge opportunity to improve selling efforts by focusing on this channel. From building brand awareness and creating an instant level of credibility to sharing case studies and highlighting references, social media is changing where the game is being played. The sales process has adapted, and so to must the way in which sellers approach it.

Sales Tools

One of the most common tools that supports and enables the sales and account management process is a customer relationship management (CRM) system. Popular examples include Salesforce and Microsoft Dynamics. Over the past several decades, even as these tools have evolved, they have experienced mixed adoption rates from sellers. Interestingly enough, Millennial sellers don't just adopt these tools, they demand them. Having grown up with technology as a part of their daily lives, they are much more fluent in the application and use of technology. By capturing efforts in a way that communicates the work they are doing alongside the work that needs to be done, a well-implemented CRM system can provide Millennials with a glorified to-do list often leveraged as their roadmap for success.

Josh Rosenberg's company, Inventus, employs a multigenerational sales force. A few years ago, Inventus installed a leading CRM system, and the results were surprising. The Millennials were naturally engaged right away and leveraged the CRM right out of the gate. His natural concern was with the Baby Boomers, who had typically viewed any new technology or tool deployment with derision. To his delight, they adopted the technology quickly and became "raving fans." They found the "tickler" function (a shortcut) for key tasks very useful and highly valued the increased visibility into their sales pipeline. His biggest challenges came from his Gen X sales reps, specifically the superstars within that particular generational grouping. They failed to adopt it, nor did they use it as part of their daily or weekly routine. We commonly find that this group feels a bit "untouchable" and sees the CRM as a big waste of time, so long as they are already hitting their numbers.

Our survey results confirmed Josh's experiences and found that Gen X uses CRM tools less than other generations: 96 percent of Millennials said that CRM was either "important" or "extremely important" in helping them achieve their sales goals, compared to 83 percent of Baby Boomers and only 69 percent of Gen Xers. Similarly, Eric Middleton says that Gen X understands that the data can provide unwanted "visibility" and attention to their sales pipeline and activity, and that, as a result, they can be "cagey" about the information they share.

We have also seen companies deploy technologies to their sales teams that overshoot the needs by being too technologically sophisticated. A large North American equipment rental company enabled their entire sales force with iPads equipped with built-in custom apps and sales tools. These apps contain customer information, a company overview, and product presentations, and enable seamless online ordering. Unfortunately, customer meetings were held on construction sites with less sophisticated buyers. For these buyers, the fancy "toys" are not going to move the needle and, worse, they could cause a bad distraction altogether. To their credit, the sales reps in this example were able to exercise Generational Flexibility and determine when and where to use their iPads so as to not disrupt their selling efforts and relationships with key decision-makers.

It is clear that all generations feel that technology is critical to success. As companies continue to build and expand multigenerational sales teams, they must invest and adopt technologies, tools, and training that many younger employees can leverage and also expect to enable their success. For all generations, but especially with Gen X, sales technologies must provide immediate value to the seller (such as dynamic content that can be created by the seller for a specific customer meeting) and not just simply report sales activity and pipeline/forecast status.

. . . .

Enablement and People

Even with incredible technologies being developed and released every year, most complex B2B sales teams still require the "right" people—those with a mix of experience, education, capability, and drive to win business. Many sales managers and company executives tell us that their number-one challenge is "talent" and their organization's ability to recruit, onboard, and develop top talent. Almost every client we work with is trying to address some or all of these problems with varying degrees of success. Let's look at each of these three areas.

Recruiting

The first place to start when recruiting for sales roles is to define the capabilities and experience required to successfully implement the sales process. Sales leaders, along with their HR business partners, must also determine the type of employee that will fit well within the culture of the organization, including the generational mix as a function of the experience and the required skills to be successful in the role.

In a discussion with Lisa Redekop, director of specialist sales operations and strategies for Gartner UK, she described Gartner's pragmatic approach to recruiting and onboarding. By sourcing recent college graduates exclusively for starter inside sales roles, Gartner hires candidates without ingrained "habits" preferring to develop them internally. The company has found that candidates with more experience (and therefore habits) are more difficult to engage, and employing them would likely lead to higher costs and increased turnover. Gartner is extremely forthcoming with its young sales candidates about the opportunity for career progression. Employees who begin in the inside sales role should plan on a five- to seven-year development path with promotion through roles with increasing responsibilities. Program participants will build skills and business acumen through high volumes of inside sales–based activities before being promoted to an inside sales manager. After spending five to seven years learning the business, employees will typically transition to major accounts, but the move is harder and more competitive than many other companies because Gartner recruits outside the firm for the major accounts role as well. They really have to be good to make the next move up.

The Millennials Gartner is recruiting have a desire to see a defined career and development path over time. In the end, this clearly defined career path helps set expectations between the individual and the organization. Though not contractually binding, a formal program indicates a commitment. It's when the commitment isn't honored that we see turn-over rise.

This approach requires three things:

1. The organization must have a very clear picture for the type of individual they are looking to recruit: open to learning the Gartner sales approach and eager to progress through an aggressive career path.

2. A substantial investment of time and money must be allocated to train these new hires.

3. A continued commitment associated with ongoing professional development and career pathing.

For some organizations, hiring the right candidate to fit a specific role, without consideration for career progression, is often deemed more cost effective. It may be cheaper, but remember that most humans like to be challenged. If not sufficiently challenged, individuals may become demotivated, complacent, and unhappy, leading to predictable turnover.

Onboarding

Once you have recruited the right talent, assimilating those individuals into your organization is just as important. We often see feeble attempts and over-engineered programs that fall short of the mark. When companies get onboarding right, they put a lot of thought into what types of roles they are onboarding and the profile of employees in those roles, and they consider the time and structure needed to make the program as effective as possible. We strongly suggest companies do not confuse onboarding with "orientation" training. Onboarding is much deeper than getting your badge, learning policies, and being issued a computer. We will be addressing the topic of onboarding in Chapter 5, but it's important to realize the value associated with a well-crafted and executed onboarding program.

Sales Skill Development

The last topic to look at with regard to enablement and people is sales skills development, which we detail more thoroughly in Chapter 6. We have found that organizations that provide relevant training materials and experiences, tailored to specific generational needs and learning styles, have an opportunity to develop talent while keeping individuals engaged and driving increased levels of adoption and retention. This is especially true for Millennials, who in some cases enter sales positions with little formal training and preparation. The ability to develop sellers' skills in a segmented, but targeted, fashion can be a huge win and will be a point of competitive differentiation for sales organizations and their teams.

Metrics and Management

Sales organizations require metrics in order to effectively manage the business in the short and long term. Key performance indicators (KPIs), both leading and lagging, must be put in place so that success may be measured, and certain behaviors can be identified and either replicated or remediated. Metrics can be applied broadly to sellers or specifically when managing changes to any of the areas defined by our "Way of Sales" model.

Sales Metrics

In sales there is only one question that matters: Did you hit your number? It goes without saying, however, that sales is also about relationships, communication, and other intangible areas that aren't as black and white as a yes or no answer. Most sales organizations adeptly track both leading (e.g., sales pipeline, sales activity) and lagging (e.g., win rates, sales cycle lengths, average deal size) indicators to monitor and manage their business. Think about the earnings estimates of a publicly traded company: A key component is the predicated revenue, based in large part by the sales pipeline and forecast for a given time period. This data provides an opportunity to build excitement and momentum, and is often used as a key motivating force for sellers. Some companies are gathering data to understand their workforce: tracking tenure, movement, performance evaluations, and attrition, as well as other qualitative data to gauge engagement and find ways to increase productivity. This qualitative data will often point to areas where companies could improve.

Sales metrics, quotas, and KPIs are interesting to explore in relation to generational nuances. Earlier we introduced you to Eric Middleton from Gladly, who shared an interesting story about Gen X being less likely to want transparency associated with reporting sales numbers, opportunity, and quota achievement. With extensive experience managing Millennial sellers, Eric noticed that they are very open and transparent with their sales numbers and forecasts, even if they are performing well below expectations. He also shared that his more experienced sellers, usually Gen Xers, will hold back and prefer to not openly share information with peers or managers. He believes that his Millennial sellers are less concerned about the consequences of having a bad pipeline or a poor forecast, and instead see reporting as a way to feed their need for an open dialogue with management. They will get attention from reporting, they want the open dialogue in order to perpetuate development, and it gives them a chance to be heard. Eric does stress that this often puts the Millennial sellers in a "be careful what you ask for" dilemma, as they can find themselves seated with very senior leaders explaining poor performance. Because of their experience, Gen X sellers have a better understanding of how management uses these reports, how to sandbag (under estimate sales), and how to avoid being noticed—until they close a large deal and want all of the recognition and attention under the sun. The lesson is that different groups attach different meaning to metrics, quotas, and KPIs. It is important to consider the composition of the sales team when determining the frequency and reporting of key metrics. Too much measurement can be just as troublesome as not enough.

Sales Team Performance and Turnover

Sales team turnover is also an area worth considering. Exit interviews rarely identify the real reasons for turnover unless the employee has a real axe to grind. What should be reviewed are why sellers are leaving, or being asked to leave, and identifying whether any of the areas of concern can be proactively addressed. Generational nuances tend to have a cause and effect relationship, especially when it comes to interactions within an organization. In Chapter 5, we'll take a closer look at causes for turnover by generation, such as:

- No opportunities to get promoted.
- Not being challenged by current role.
- Limited training/development opportunities.
- Being offered a better compensation package.
- Being offered a better title.
- Little collaboration across the team.
- Boring work culture.
- Bad leadership.
- Poor reputation of the company.
- Lack of flexibility (e.g., time, location, etc.).

These are just a few of the reasons turnover can occur in a sales environment and each one holds different weight for sellers based on their generations.

• •

Assessing Your Organization

Assessments can be challenging and often require a frank look in the mirror. It's like the Stockdale Paradox from Jim Collins's *Good to Great*: "You must never confuse faith that you will prevail in the end—which you can never afford to lose—with the discipline to confront the most brutal facts of your current reality, whatever they might be."[4] Of course, an assessment of these four areas isn't nearly as extreme, but it will provide you with an indication of what's working well and areas that require attention and investment.

There are some common areas to look out for as companies analyze the possible impacts of generational nuances. Remember: not everything needs attention and may require something as simple as an open dialogue between two people. At the very least, it is worth looking at the dynamic between sales professionals and sales leaders, the customer interaction, and especially talent development. These areas can often be referred to as "the front lines" of the Generational Imperative and may require immediate attention.

By being tuned in to the areas that require tweaking, organizations can focus on actions that can provide an immediate benefit without over-engineering every aspect of the business. A client of ours specializing in consumer packaged goods had all the right intentions when it set out to deal with the generational differences impacting its organization. This company typically employed younger team members in sales and marketing, and hired more tenured individuals to occupy senior leadership positions. The company began addressing the problem by focusing on mentoring, career path programs, and making senior staff well aware of generational nuances in a productive way. After seeing such a positive impact, it began to update value propositions, messaging, collateral, and commercial communications. The company over-engineered its marketing messages and TV campaigns, which, when launched, felt forced and uncomfortable. Remember that not every message requires a hip, generational twist. Look at how many ads today include a Millennial couple posting pictures or a Baby Boomer using the term *selfie*. Not every single thread of an organization requires attention; identify the areas where improvement can be made and prioritize those that have the largest impact on things like retention, customer acquisition, and overall employee productivity.

In the next three chapters, we will focus specifically on recruiting and onboarding, sales skill development, sales coaching, and performance management. As the assessment indicates, we believe tweaking these areas will have the biggest impact within most sales organizations. We have touched on some of these areas already, but we will dive into much more detail and provide additional insights for how organizations should approach these concepts.

5

Recruiting and Onboarding Multigenerational Sales Talent

"Every new generation is a fresh invasion of savages."
—Hervey Allen, American poet, biographer, and novelist (1889–1949)

All organizations struggle with talent, especially sales teams. High-growth companies struggle to find enough sellers. Underperforming companies struggle to find qualified sellers that fit the mold. Stable companies, with tenured employees, struggle to have enough turnover to bring in new blood. These are just a few of the problems companies are facing as it relates to finding and building talent.

For recruiting and onboarding within the sales organization, we believe the challenge is bigger than just making the organization more "hip" for a new crop of sales professionals entering their first corporate posting. According to our research, it takes on average between four and 12 months to ramp a new hire to effectively sell a company's products or services. Baby Boomer sales professionals, with decades of experience, are leaving roles to retire, and many organizations can't or won't consider replacing them with sellers who are equally as experienced but often just as expensive. To make matters worse, when lower-level sales professionals are hired, they are not afforded the same training these tenured professionals have acquired over the years. As a sales leader, the problem is that you have replaced the experienced individual with a less-expensive but seemingly less-effective seller. Remember that by 2025, almost half of the U.S. workforce will be Millennials, which will significantly impact sales and sales leadership.[1] The approach that sales organizations undertake to locate, hire, and onboard the right talent must adapt.

Talent challenges will only become more difficult as the reality settles in that a third of employed Millennials are actively looking for a job and are projected to stay with an employer for an average of two years.[2] Plenty of sales organizations can barely approach getting a territory up to peak profitability in less than two years. What does the crystal ball tell us? This problem is not going away anytime soon, and even companies that find stability for a period of time must remain vigilant for the pending outflow of talent and inflow of new team members. As we found in our research, when describing the top-10 characteristics of sellers, loyalty to a company or organization is a top characteristic of both the Baby Boomers and Gen X, but is found in the bottom three for Millennials. Simply put, this movie will replay itself for a long time to come and most likely even accelerate.

Before we continue, we offer several disclaimers: We are not a recruiting firm. We do have relationships with, and have reached out to, recruiting professionals as we constructed the advice found in this chapter. We also refer specifically to roles in sales and sales leadership, as this is our area of expertise. We are not referring to the recruiting and onboarding of other roles within organizations, although generational research supports many of these findings across other functional areas. Generational nuances should be considered when hiring people for sales and sales leadership roles. However, as we previously mentioned, the best approach is to focus on skills, roles, facts, outcomes, interviewing, and selection, not simply generational groups or age, which in some cases can be discriminatory.

Recruiting a Multigenerational Sales Force

The steps involved in recruiting a multigenerational sales force are essentially the same as those used to recruit anyone to an organization. For small companies and teams, we recommend a logical and disciplined path for acquiring talent. This requires careful planning and analysis before interviewing potential candidates. Based on our own experience and through our work and conversations with professional recruiters, a well-defined recruiting process should follow these five steps:

1. **Determine what you need.** This involves determining what roles are to be filled, clear role definitions, desired skill sets, and required levels of experience. It is critical to implement a well-conceived competency model to identify the core knowledge, skills, and abilities required to be successful in the role. If you plan on offering a robust sales training program post-onboarding, perhaps you are able to hire sellers that are less experienced. The same holds true in the inverse scenario, in which an organization is seeking to employ a seller for a major account that requires significant negotiating abilities and industry knowledge.

2. **Identify what your candidates want in a company.** Depending upon who is the best fit for the open role(s), companies have to consider whether or not they can realistically attract and acquire the right talent. This involves marketing the company in ways that attract the right candidates. By profiling the ideal candidate, organizations can more effectively appeal to their motivations for joining your organization. For example, a Baby Boomer may be less worried about career pathing versus the promise of extensive healthcare coverage and life insurance; conversely, a Millennial may seek a more open, informal, and collaborative working environment.

3. **Interview for the right fit.** Most companies, either directly or through an agency, interview potential candidates. The key is to conduct behavioral-based interviews, and focus on learning if the candidate possesses the requisite skills and knowledge and/or can quickly close any gaps through the on-boarding process. Understand your candidate's preferences and tailor your approach to meet their expectations accordingly. Generational characteristics are a great starting point, but as we outlined in Chapter 1, people are "blended." Hiring managers must look beyond generalizations and clichés, and focus on the candidate to confirm motivations. If Step 1 is done properly, the interview process and candidate discussions becomes more of a validation and less of a guessing game. Think about the last time you had to replace a star seller. What made them so effective? Did customer satisfaction surveys ever provide insight into what this seller did or did not do? When customers have preferences for how they expect your organization to service their needs, it's often important to align the attributes of a past seller to that of their replacement. This makes the transition much easier for the most important person, the customer.

4. **Make a compelling offer and close the "sale."** This is rather obvious, but there are a couple headlines to consider. Reference and align with the candidate's motivations (as much as possible) through the offer and the messaging used to communicate the offer. For example, if career development is a priority, highlight the onboarding process and opportunities for continued development and mobility within the organization. Move swiftly through the process, and be sure to set expectations for what the candidate can expect. Most candidates understand that they are not the only candidate being interviewed, but do not draw the process out. Establishing a time line, especially for Millennials, is a good idea and helps to set expectations for an audience that is used to instant gratification.

5. **Develop a strong onboarding plan.** Recruiting the right people is half the battle. Ensuring that new hires are properly onboarded is just as important as getting them in the door. This is about putting people through a structured and consistent program that shortens the learning curve, defines the desired culture within the organization, and seeks to expedite revenue results. This is not "orientation training." Onboarding is a huge undertaking for some organizations and should be treated as a recruiting asset in many cases. It should be communicated in the recruiting process, especially for Millennials, who in our survey showed a desire for robust training programs compared with other generations. Setting expectations for what success looks like only helps provide employees, from every generation, with the information they need to recognize how their contribution ultimately impacts the health of their team and that of the overall organization.

This is not an exhaustive list and omits key components of the process such as background and reference checks. Our intent is not to outline a fully complete checklist for a recruiting process but simply to highlight several key areas that we feel must be considered alongside the topic of generational diversity. Let us now look closer at each one of these steps as we prepare to positively impact the recruiting and onboarding process.

Determine What You Need

Our recommended first step in the recruiting process is to clearly define what is required for success in the position, which includes the following::

- The key requirements of the role. What skills or qualities must the candidate embody in order to be successful?

- Information and results from current or similar positions within the company. What has worked and not worked before?

- The life-cycle stage of the business (startup, growth, stable, decline, recovery). Is the focus on the quantity of feet on the street or the quality of a few key roles?

- The company's product(s) or service(s) and the corresponding sales process. Are you looking for a high-volume, transactional candidate or an experienced consultative sales person?

- The company's reporting structure (e.g., hierarchical vs. flat vs. matrixed), which helps understand how well potential candidates can operate independently.

- The remote or flexible office nature of the role and company.

This list of considerations can be extensive, but we often see companies skip this step and end up failing to bring the right people onboard. Putting pen to paper in this way provides a solid foundation for effective interview questioning, sets expectations for the role, and creates measures by which the new hire can be reviewed to determine effectiveness in the role.

Thinking about seller attributes that ring true to most managers, we posed this question within our Generational Selling Survey. For sales managers looking to hire a new candidate we asked respondents for the relative importance of each of the following characteristics when hiring a new seller:

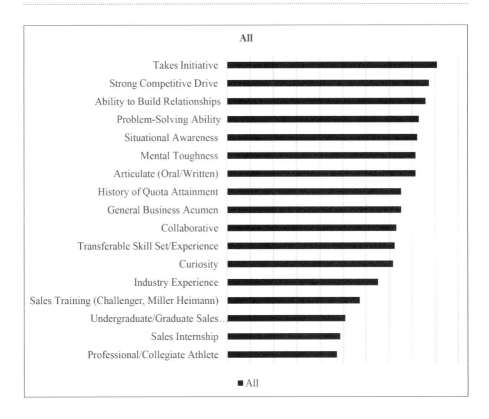

All

Takes Initiative	
Strong Competitive Drive	
Ability to Build Relationships	
Problem-Solving Ability	
Situational Awareness	
Mental Toughness	
Articulate (Oral/Written)	
History of Quota Attainment	
General Business Acumen	
Collaborative	
Transferable Skill Set/Experience	
Curiosity	
Industry Experience	
Sales Training (Challenger, Miller Heimann)	
Undergraduate/Graduate Sales..	
Sales Internship	
Professional/Collegiate Athlete	

■ All

As you can see, managers are interviewing for drive and soft skills more than experience and education. Although most companies typically have minimum requirements for educational levels, Monster.com eludes to the fact that requiring industry experience screams, "we're too lazy to train you." They explain that companies must "drop 'experience' from the list of sales recruiting requirements and look for motivated people who can come into your organization and find an environment in which to excel."[3] This isn't so much detrimental to the Gen X and Boomer sellers who do possess experience, so much as it is the markets response to the fact that so many new hires are, in fact, lesser experienced Millennials.

In theory, and in practice, this concept of training to the job holds water. Mike Rosenburg echoed this sentiment when he explained the seller qualities that seem to resonate at his company. Healthgrades, he said, is "flexible and open on hiring—and have hired both inexperienced and experienced sales professionals. Rather than focusing on experience, we mainly look for sales aptitude and likability factor." Though likability may not be the easiest thing to measure, especially with so many equal opportunity and anti-discrimination laws to keep in mind, determining the best fit for your organization prior to interviewing candidates will improve your recruiting process.

Identify What Your Candidates Want in a Company

Understanding what might be motivating a candidate is a critical step, especially for industries in which finding great sellers can be extremely competitive. It's all about the "brand" companies seek to portray when trying to attract the best talent. This brand, or perception, is what we refer to as the Employee Value Proposition.

In 2015, we created our own Employee Value Proposition at Symmetrics Group. Through facilitated working sessions, our team clearly defined and articulated our company values, which were based on preferred working styles, professional motivations, and our mutually shared desire to help our clients become more effective. Capturing these values allowed us to more effectively align our priorities alongside key motivating factors that appeal to interview candidates, resulting in alignment and cultural fit.

The way an individual perceives a company's description of the job opportunity, and all associated benefits, is heavily influenced by that individual's generation. Companies must think about whom they are targeting and how their ideal candidates will perceive the brand, the culture, or both. We recently worked with a client who has office locations across the United States. This company, founded in the 1960s, has historically attracted a relatively young and inexperienced sales team, which they then develop by perpetuating their proven selling methodology. Increasingly, as the Millennials have become the latest cohort to enter the workforce, the company began finding it difficult to attract this generation, given the perceived culture of the company. The overall brand and office aesthetics had not been revamped in decades. What was once considered fresh and fun for Baby Boomers just entering the workforce, now felt stale and antiquated.

We are not saying that an interior design overhaul is required to attract Millennial talent, but it is important to realize that your organization carries a perception. How people view your brand speaks volumes about the type of individuals who might want to work there. Even within a single industry, perceptions draw out different motivations. Take the energy industry as an example. An energy utility maintains the pipes and wires associated with getting energy to homes and businesses. It's somewhat recession-proof in that every household and business requires energy to operate. These organizations tend to employ "lifers," with many staying at the organization for their entire career. On the other hand, we can have a renewable energy company focused on cutting-edge solar technology. This fast-paced organization attracts a younger cohort, mainly Millennials looking to be at the forefront of an industry and Gen Xers seeking to push the status quo.

Not being able to hire the talent required to do the job meant that the organization we are referring to was unable to meet forecasted growth targets. The company is now overhauling its offices and brand, but is still operating with reduced headcount and trailing revenue expectations. Note that this business result is not driven by customers or the market, but by the plain and simple competition for talent.

When developing a job description for an open position, most companies look for some degree of experience but prefer not to hire candidates *too* late in their careers. This can be a very slippery slope, and companies must be careful not to create ads for open roles so limiting that people automatically deselect themselves (e.g., 20+ years of experience required, seasoned sales professionals only, extensive history of a successful track record required).

It is amazing that some of these companies shy away from people they sense may be late in their careers because they assume the candidates are not as "hungry" as they once were. In conversations with multiple recruiters, we were told that what companies are really interviewing for is the exact same thing we introduced earlier in this book: place in life. Employers are looking for people who have "can't-fail DNA" because they have a home, a family, cars, schools to pay for, and the need for substantial income. This translates into built-in motivation, and a person from any generation can fit this bill. Our recruiting contacts tell us that the style of interview questions employers ask are now less about skills/technical abilities and more about place in life, culture fit, and a proven track record of success.

· ·

Interviewing for the Right Fit

We interviewed Larry Nettles, prior head of sales development for PGI, about recruiting best practices and determining the fit for candidate identification and placement. PGI employs a large sales force that includes a mix of sellers from each generation. Despite successfully reducing the turnover among their tenured sellers from 42 to 17 percent in 2014, PGI still needed to onboard a large number of entry-level sellers each year in order to support their growth objectives. Larry worked with his recruiting and human resources teams to design a new program focused on hiring entry level, Millennial sellers based on fit.

Understanding that Millennials work more collaboratively than other generations, PGI designed a virtual panel-based group interview process whereby three to four PGI hiring managers could interview three to four entry-level sales candidates at the same time. There were several benefits to this approach. First, the program helped PGI scale their interview efforts by saving time and money by interviewing several candidates at once and using virtual meeting technology instead of flying each candidate in for an interview. The second benefit was that it gave the entry-level candidates the perception that PGI was on the forefront of technology—something important to many Millennials pursuing jobs right out of college and also an important PGI brand attribute. The third, and probably most important, benefit to using the group interview approach was what PGI was able to learn about each of the candidates.

During the interview process, the PGI hiring managers were less interested in how candidates answered each question, but were more focused on how the candidates interacted with one another. They categorized each candidate into one of three profiles: confrontational, aggressive, or assertive. PGI wanted to hire candidates who were assertive, but not confrontational or aggressive, in a group setting. Because PGI strives to build a collaborative and collegial work environment, it was essential to make sure the entry-level candidates were the right fit based on the culture. PGI's assessment of a candidate's cultural fit held more weight than other traditional assessment criteria, such as education level or sales experience. PGI's entry-level sales recruiting strategy anchored on the philosophy that if they could get the cultural fit right, they could teach the new hire their sales methodology.

We also interviewed Monica Stone, a professional recruiter with more than 20 years of experience who has supported our own firm's recruiting process. She was intrigued by the fact that we were asking questions about this topic, as she feels so many of her clients have neglected to modernize their approach when searching for and acquiring new talent. She explained that the types of questions she asks to qualify candidates do not change, but the responses help her understand and validate their motivating factors beyond the preconceived notions she has given more obvious attributes like age. Based on how organizations define fit, these questions, and their correlated answers, help her qualify candidates very early in the conversation:

- Where do you live?
- What is your willingness to travel and/or relocate?
- What is your current state of employment?
- What is your tolerance for change?
- What is your compensation history and/or monetary requirements?
- Who can provide references?
- What research have you done on the potential hiring company?

On the surface, these may seem like fluff, "get to know you" questions, but the answers to these questions help recruiters and organizations alike understand candidates' "place in life" and validate their generational "slice of pie."

We would like to offer a bit more thought on what we mean by behavior-based interviewing. This is a technique in which the interviewer does not ask obvious leading questions, but more situational style questions that force the candidate to think and provide a real story or situation that answers the question. The interviewer gains insight in to how well they can think on their feet and provide a solid answer—a huge skill required for sales success. Let's look at a few examples that can help interviewers uncover key skills and experiences from candidates of any generation:

- Tell me about a time when you collaborated with a team to land a sale or complete a detailed project. (Can the candidate work with a broad team?)

- Describe a time when you had to get creative to move a deal forward. (Can they move a sale ahead and solve problems?)

- Describe a time when the coaching you received from a leader helped you get better results. (Are they coachable?)

- Describe a specific customer that took you a long time to crack and finally get the relationship started. (Can they deal with long sales cycles?)

- Describe what parts of the sales process you feel you can improve upon. (Do they understand a sales process and have awareness of their development areas?)

- Tell me about a customer that you do not click with and why. (Do they have awareness of style? Are they flexible?)

These are examples of the conversations that hiring managers should start with sellers, from any generation, to get a view into their behaviors. These types of interview questions keep a conversation flowing, a key sales skill, and limit the use of obvious answer questions that yield no insight into behavior. Our suggestion is to list the skills and behaviors you are interviewing for and then craft behavior-based questions that help you creatively shape the right conversation. And remember: If candidates seek clarification to your questions, it shows they are listening and thinking about how to give you what you want. Hire them! They can think on their feet!

Make a Compelling Offer and Close the "Sale"

What defines an "attractive offer with compelling benefits" is constantly evolving. Organizations that believe an offer that was compelling 10 years ago will attract today's top talent will be very disappointed. Companies today must consider factors like flexible work schedules, vacation policies, relocation packages, and signing bonuses. In fact, a number of companies now are even offering unlimited vacation and maternity/paternity leave. Although it is still early to see if these will be enduring trends, the fact remains that individuals are looking for more work/life balance, flexible hours, and policies that were unheard of 10 to 15 years ago.

In our research, we asked sellers to indicate the importance of various benefits when contemplating a new sales role. We found that for sellers, across all generations, the top two most attractive benefits were the same:

1. Competitive base salary.
2. High variable compensation.

When we got to benefits number three and beyond, we started noticing some differences in what was compelling to the sellers from different generations. Gen Xers and Baby Boomers ranked items such as health insurance and paid time off (PTO) at the top of their lists; Millennials prioritized other things, like compelling career paths and flexible working hours. Even more interesting, Millennial sellers ranked "philanthropic opportunities" second to last on their list, which debunks the perception that this is a top attraction driver for all Millennials.

Millennials	Gen X	Baby Boomers
Competitive Base Salary	Competitive Base Salary	Competitive Base Salary
High Variable Comp. Potential	High Variable Comp. Potential	High Variable Comp. Potential
Compelling Career Path	Competitive Health Insurance	Competitive Health Insurance
Flexible Working Hours	Competitive Paid Time Off Policy	Competitive Paid Time Off Policy
Competitive Paid Time Off Policy	Flexible Working Hours	Pension and/or Retirement Options
Robust Training Program	Pension and/or Retirement Options	Flexible Working Hours
Competitive Health Insurance	Compelling Career Path	Robust Training Program
Pension and/or Retirement Options	Robust Training Program	Social Work Culture
Tuition Reimbursement	Social Work Culture	Compelling Career Path
Social Work Culture	Parental and Child Care Benefits	Cross-Training Rotational Programs
Cross-Training Rotational Programs	Cross-Training Rotational Programs	Entertainment Budget
Entertainment Budget	Philanthropic Opportunities	Philanthropic Opportunities
Parental and Child Care Benefits	Tuition Reimbursement	Tuition Reimbursement
Philanthropic Opportunities	Entertainment Budget	Parental and Child Care Benefits
Access to Low Interest Loans	Access to Low Interest Loans	Access to Low Interest Loans

From our conversations with hiring managers and recruiters focused on finding the right sales professionals, we validated the age-old assumption that Millennials care less about monetary requirements and more about the "feel good" effect. It's not surprising given compensation expectations for most sales-related roles that individuals looking for this type of opportunity are likely in it for the money. As many as half of Millennial candidates are asking for signing bonuses and relocation expenses. With this in mind, some important considerations seem universally applicable to candidates: flexible schedules, ability to work at home some of the time, attractive benefits, and evidence of a healthy culture that allows for work/life balance.

Today, candidates are showing up more researched and prepared, and they expect to learn more about the role, the culture, and overall fit, not just about the company. Generational nuances are part of this mix, but we must advise that companies and candidates keep an open mind to possibilities and consider using the advice we have already provided. Do not generalize based on generations and let observable behavior drive your decisions.

A plug for outsourcing: We strongly suggest companies consider deploying professional recruiters in their efforts, even if they have their own internal staff. Recruiting firms that specialize in specific areas, such as collegiate athletes or experienced professionals focused on C-Suite appointments, understand the needs of their generationally distinct clients. They understand what organizations need and the motivating factors of potential candidates. Leveraging them can elevate the entire staffing process by making it more competitive as people seek to produce results. Professional recruiters know the best ways to find candidates, get them engaged, and stay within the lines defined by the organization, based on fit. It is safe to conclude that the game has changed and generational nuances are in the mix.

Develop a Strong Onboarding Plan

Onboarding people from multiple generations is a hot topic in most companies today. As more people exit key roles and new people come in the door, companies must figure out how to get them up to speed and productive as quickly as possible. We interviewed Evan Steiner, a senior sales leader who spent 11 years focused on sales effectiveness at Constellation

Energy. Evan has led many sales teams over his career and shared some of his perspectives on the potential onboarding can have on an organization's success. Evan explained that "Top sales talent is not bought. It is grown through immersing people within the culture: skills, product knowledge, and understanding how to navigate the organization can only be acquired through strong onboarding and ongoing training." Highlighting something that we feel most companies miss, Evan described how many companies hire or "buy" experience with the hope that people will succeed based upon a past track record. The assumption is that people will figure out the skills they need to be successful and assimilate into the culture on their own. These companies fail to teach these important attributes as part of the onboarding program, and instead only focus on "orientation" activities such as basic product knowledge and administrative activities like getting their badge photo taken and learning the locations of the restrooms and fire exits.

According to our research, it takes on average between four and 12 months for a majority of sales professionals to ramp a new hire to effectively sell a company's product or services. Onboarding should not be "a quick hit." Instead, companies must be prepared to invest the time and resources needed to bring new sellers up to speed. By setting expectations around goals and the organizations culture, onboarding can have a positive and lasting impact on a seller's ability to assimilate into the organization by understanding their role in it. This is extremely important for Millennials who are seeking to understand where their efforts fit into the bigger picture and for Gen X and Baby Boomer sellers who find it helpful to have an organization acknowledge their level of experience as a sign of respect versus eluding to the fact that they will "soon be put out to pasture" (which we have actually heard uttered—no pun intended). In our survey of sellers and sales leaders, a majority responded that onboarding should run between four to 12 months, with the exception of Millennials, 38 percent of whom said that onboarding should take one to three months.

This may correlate to the Millennial expectation that they should be able to learn the skills within a short period of time. Because of this, companies should ensure that onboarding is mostly completed within six months, especially if they employ a high percentage of Millennials in their sales organizations.

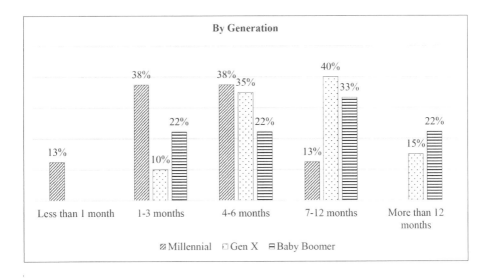

One of the biggest mistakes we see companies make with onboarding is allowing a sales leader or senior sales reps to patch together a program comprised of a collection of "training documents" and stick them online or in a binder with the intention of training new employees. As well-intentioned as the self-appointed sales training may be, daily responsibilities will inhibit them from providing the value that new hires desperately seek. Onboarding should be considered an investment. As such, dedicated resources should be assigned if they are available.

Another mistake is perpetuating a self-guided onboarding approach. So is a half-hearted attempt to pair a new-hire with an experienced seller and rely on "peer coaching." Both fail as priorities shift focus and incentives continue to be revenue-oriented versus based on peer aptitude.

An effective onboarding program should include, at the very least, the following elements and should be supported by an implementation strategy that manages generational nuances in an effective way:

- Role clarity and job descriptions.

- Reporting structure and expectations.

- Product/service training.

- HR admin (payroll, benefits, policies, equipment, security, etc.)

Often, companies end their onboarding here, leaving the rest for on-the-job development. This is a big mistake. Instead companies should include the following in order to shorten new hire ramp to effectiveness:

- A review of the company's value and culture (what makes a successful employee).

- A plan for ongoing shadowing and in-the-field and/or on-the-phone coaching.

- An established 1:1 cadence for development with tenured sales staff/sales leaders.

- A healthy balance of traditional training and on-the-job coaching/feedback from prospects or customer-facing interactions.

- Peer-led training on the use of the relevant sales tools (CRM, marketing materials, presentation building, etc.).

- Industry and product/solution overviews that provide content that new hires can readily use and adapt in their customer-facing conversations.

- A review of the company's career path options and an open dialogue around the new hire's career aspirations.

From a multigenerational perspective, a key to creating a successful onboarding program is assessing the needs of the sales force in the aggregate. By leveraging the competency model, developed to support effective recruiting practices, organizations can assess what trainings are required prior to determining how best to deliver each piece of education. Classroom training may be overkill for some more tenured sellers, yet it's exactly what is needed for others. The safe decision is to prepare for both and have the courses ready, and consider what requirements may be applicable should you have a large influx of new hires from a particular generation.

Millennial Sales Onboarding (6 Months)

Back in the 1980s and 1990s, many of the leading companies in the United States offered significant development programs for sales new hires. IBM, Xerox, Wang, Hewlett Packard, Toshiba, P&G, and many more provided their sales new hires with anywhere from a six-week to 18-month expansive training program designed to teach foundational selling methods and skills. In many cases, the new hires had to successfully complete the program before ever speaking to an actual customer.

Today, many of these same companies have dramatically scaled back these programs and have outsourced much of the training and development. Alumni from Xerox and IBM along with Neil Rackham, who consulted with these firms, essentially created the global sales training industry. As a sales new hire, imagine a situation in which you graduated from college with a degree in anthropology and after a couple years realized the only way you could pay back your student loans was to get a job with a higher earning potential. But wait—you have never sold a thing, and in your new sales role, the company wants to start you with mid-market-size customers who spend between $100,000 and $500,000 per year. You are going to call almost exclusively on information technology (IT) leaders in medium-sized companies. You have never been taught any sales skills. What exactly are typical sales skills? A short list includes:

- Planning (territory, account, opportunity).
- Prospecting (phone, email, social media).
- Issue/need diagnosis and discovery.

- Presentation.
- Closing (objection handling and negotiation).
- Collaboration, both internally and externally, with business partners and customers.
- Communication (written and verbal).

Putting yourself in the shoes of a new Millennial seller, the program must be fun, engaging, and something companies want their employees to tell their friends about. It used to be a point of pride when a young seller completed the program, especially in the case of IBM. Companies looking to do the same should implement the following structure, aiming to wrap the program up by the end of month six:

1. Industry and vertical market training (especially if they lack this).
2. Company culture assimilation (meet others like them); career paths/planning for the future.
3. Soft skill development; instructor-led and distance learning.
4. Shadowing/field rides.
5. 1:1 development with tenured sales staff/sales leaders.
6. Structured ongoing feedback.
7. Training on CRM, tools, sales tools.

Gen X Sales Onboarding (12 Months)

Seventy-five percent of Gen Xers told us that new hires should ramp to effectiveness within 12 months. Because Gen X sellers will likely have more experience, and will likely privately or publicly challenge approaches, we believe a longer onboarding approach makes sense. The following approach will provide a good foundation when seeking to meet the needs of this generation:

1. 1:1 development with tenured sales staff/sales leaders.

2. Shadowing/field training.

3. Industry and vertical market training; company culture assimilation.

4. Soft skill development; instructor-led and distance learning.

5. Training on CRM, tools, sales tools.

6. Career paths; planning for the future.

7. Structured ongoing feedback.

Don't be alarmed: The modules are intentionally the same, but the order is different. Because these sellers will likely have relatively more experience to draw on, it makes sense to get them in the field and fully engaged faster. This allows organizations to validate applicable skills and gives sellers the ability to decide on their own what learning may be required. It is important to let a more experienced rep draw their own conclusions versus forcing training on them that is not relevant and take their eye off the prize.

Baby Boomer Sales Onboarding (12 Months)

Fifty-five percent of Baby Boomers expect the onboarding ramp period to last up to 12 months, and we believe companies can use the same onboarding approach for Baby Boomers as they do for Gen X, while paying special attention to the reality that they have even more experiences to draw from. Companies should consider pulling forward training on CRM and sales tools if the person has not worked with technology native to their new company. They may take a few extra cycles to learn, see value, and adopt. It is also worth noting that soft skill development may meet some resistance given the depth of experience being brought to the table. You can quickly see that delivering this too early could be insulting and that it would be more powerful to let the person see other sellers in action while deciding for themselves what skills do or do not need sharpening.

• • • • • • •

There is no question that the cost associated with a formalized on-boarding program is high, though it's easy to see that the value is exponentially higher when executed effectively. For organizations that are willing and able to make the investment, it's important that they stay keenly aware of employee turnover. We will explore this concept next as we seek to ensure organizations don't let their valuable investments go to waste.

In Chapter 6, we'll focus on how to adapt training to meet the needs of a multigenerational team, which links to the knowledge and skill building components of an onboarding program. Overall, each generation finds shadowing and experiential learning as the two most valuable learning methods. Our advice is simple: good onboarding programs include a variety of learning and training methods, not just one or two.

6

Generational Considerations for Sales Skill Development

"You want to teach the next generation so they can learn a little bit faster and a little bit more so everything becomes that much better."
—Cobi Jones, former American soccer player (1970–)

Sales skill development is an important factor in the success or failure of sales professionals and leaders. We have seen this directly with our clients, from our own experience, and in current research studies. "As management shifts to younger generations, the research reveals the areas that companies can focus on to enhance skill sets, address the challenges of managing multiple generations, and retain and engage employees by understanding what workplace perks they may value most," said Karyn Twaronite, the EY Americas inclusiveness officer and a partner of Ernst & Young LLP. "While it's encouraging that Millennials are expected to significantly grow their managerial skills by 2020, the onus is on companies to also give them equitable opportunities to gain the right mentors, sponsors, career experiences, and training to capitalize on this optimism."[1]

Our experience helps us to understand how deeply generational nuances impact learning and development. During our careers in sales, consulting, and training, we have developed and delivered many types of training content and have coached thousands of sales professionals and leaders. During the past 25 years, we have observed tremendous change in content delivery and the ways in which people learn. We continue to teach sales skills to a melting pot of generations—ages ranging from between 25 and 60 years. David, a coauthor of this book, started in inside sales, where he learned and rehearsed scripts, spending countless hours training with his sales manager and a sales coach face-to-face. He and his peers were expected to spend a significant amount of time developing the skills they would need to be successful. When David transitioned to the role of trainer, he still relied heavily on face-to-face and in-the-field sales training. Today, however, there are many new options for training delivery, including facilitated remote learning, self-guided distance learning, video simulations, and on-the-job development. With so many different training options, choosing the right avenue by which to deliver your content can feel daunting.

As a part of our own ongoing development, we have both become certified in several behavioral and thinking style methodologies, such as HBDI from Hermann International and Social Styles from TRACOM. TRACOM's certification program involved a variety of different delivery channels and as Gen X learners, there were several steps that were new to us. The TRACOM training did not involve a face-to-face session and instead required David to read two books. After reviewing the assigned facilitation guide and technical documentation, David reviewed a four-hour webinar and completed an e-learning course. There may be some learners who love that TRACOM's learning path never involved a classroom, but this format challenged David to learn in a new way that felt foreign and uncomfortable. As David progressed through the certification program, he thought, *"How would a Baby Boomer learner handle this type of training?"* or *"Would a Millennial like this learning approach?"* The answer depends on what they prefer and what they are most accustomed to (and also their specific learning style, which can transcend generational groups). Learning, especially focused on sales skills, has evolved over the past 10 years. Not only have delivery options changed, but so too have learners and their expectations.

"Sales skills" refers to core selling capabilities such as prospecting for customers; researching customer information; planning for and managing a territory, account, or opportunity; business or industry acumen; effectively presenting ideas and insights; overcoming objections; negotiating agreements; and managing customer relationships. Companies may classify other "sales skills," but the fact of the matter is that different generations prefer to learn these skills in different ways. Sellers have grown up with various learning options, which has forced companies to update their "one size fits all" training approach. For the most part, sales skills require real-time or simulated human interactions, which often demand that sellers learn skills through repetitive practice. Not surprisingly, our research shows that the most effective method of training occurs through "active" learning, such as simulations, case studies, and sales call observations with a manager or fellow sellers.

Still, many companies deploy instructor-led and distance-learning options because they tend to be easier to organize, more scalable, and more cost effective. Additionally, ensuring that the quality of the content remains intact is a big consideration. Imagine one trainer explaining a process in 30 training sessions versus 30 different managers giving varied explanations to their sellers as they facilitate ride-alongs. With distance learning, it's even better: one recording, one message. Overall, the order of training preferences is similar across each of the generations, as noted here.

Ordering of Training Preferences

(1=Most Preferred; 5=Least Preferred)

	Millennial	Gen X	Baby Boomer
1.	Shadowing/Ride Along	Shadowing/Ride Along	Experiential Learning
2.	Experiential Learning	Experiential Learning	Shadowing/Ride Along
3.	Classroom Learning	Classroom Learning	Classroom Learning
4.	Self-Paced Learning	Self-Paced Learning	Self-Paced Learning
5.	Online/eLearning	Online/eLearning	Online/eLearning

Companies often establish e-learning options in lieu of face-to-face training for Millennials, given their assumed preference for online and self-paced training. Although face-to-face training may not always be feasible, this data helps to validate how sellers prefer to learn new sales skills, despite their generation.

Making Adjustments

Let's look at a few examples in which we think companies should adjust their training approach depending on the generational mix of their team. This helps to enable greater overall success rates and reduces the learning curve for people in new roles. Though we offer some considerations for teaching each generation, let's remember that these are guidelines, not rules. As we discussed in Chapter 2 with the "slice of pie" approach to generational characterizations, people often break stereotypes, and Generational Flexibility rules should be considered.

Millennial Sales Professionals Training Tips

Millennials typically think, "What has worked for my peers?" and "How can I use this immediately?" It is critical to consider whether the Millennial chose sales as a profession or if sales chose them. Many new entrants to the workforce take the sales gig as a way to get their foot in the door, not realizing the flexibility and earning potential most sales roles provide. Understanding how the seller found their way to your sales or-ganization will impact the way the seller learns, the depth of development they may need, and their willingness to heed the training.

Most Millennials have been immersed in technology their whole lives and, as a result, may struggle with both the hard and soft skills required to be effective sellers. Hard skills are teachable qualities that can be easily measured, whereas soft skills are personality-driven at-tributes that are much harder to quantify. In a recent report released by PayScale, hiring managers called out "writing proficiency as the hard skill most commonly lacking and critical thinking/problem solving as the most commonly lacking soft skill. Public speaking and attention to detail follow for the second-most-lacking hard and soft skills, respec-tively."[2] This data is daunting, given that sales largely depends on skills like writing, presenting, communication, problem-solving, and atten-tion to detail. We have yet to meet a successful sales professional who lacks these skills. Learning and development professionals must con-sider closing the hard and soft skill gaps for Millennials if they are to succeed in key roles.

Companies with a large crop of entry-level Millennial sellers should incorporate training lessons on business basics, such as how to write pro-fessional emails, how to schedule appointments, and how to spend selling time and engage with prospects and clients. These things seem obvious to those who have been in the working world for a few years, but not so much for those just entering the workforce. Graduating students are ac-customed to taking a topic and expanding upon it in a paper that is no less than 10 double-spaced pages. They graduate and all of a sudden their boss wants the facts in as few words as possible. Giving attention to these over-looked skills will ensure that the adjustment are as seamless as possible.

In addition to business basics, new Millennial graduates should re-ceive a crash course on topics such as organizational hierarchies and the C-Suite, the budgeting process, and how to accurately read and under-stand a profit and loss statement. A baseline understanding of these top-ics is essential for sellers looking to connect with customers and having situational awareness of both business drivers and buyer motivations. Ian Walch, a Millennial working for a large U.S. energy provider, explained the crux of the problem to us. He noted, "Undergraduate courses may or may not prepare you as a seller. Aside from a financial planning course, which provided good acumen for B2B selling and a marketing course focused on segmentation and targeting, there were relatively no sales-specific curriculums." Ian did have the opportunity to complete a one-credit course on a Saturday that focused on B2B selling but lacked the desired learning that would have otherwise reinforced how best to position products and services directly to customers.

Sellers fortunate enough to be exposed to some level of education prior to starting their career, as Ian was, will undoubtedly have a leg up on their fellow new hires. The vast majority of new sellers are left to figure out these hard and soft skills on their own, often leading to frustration and deciding too quickly to leave sales when they could have otherwise been successful. While interning at Bloomberg in New York City, one of our Symmetrics Group colleagues was required to spend the first four weeks of the program in the classroom. All sales interns were put through a sales boot camp. They learned how to update a physical resume and curate a more appropriate personal brand online, were tasked with creating emails and PowerPoints to hone communication and presentation skills, and were even coached on physical appearance and workplace-appropriate attire and behavior. When asked, the individual cited the obvious benefits these lessons provided while also indicating that it meant a lot to her. The time the company took to assimilate young interns and new hires provided a sense of camaraderie, not just between the fellow interns but with the sales force at large. It was as if you knew that everyone had been in your shoes before and that seasoned sellers understand what it is like. So often these emotions are either ignored in their entirety or swept under the rug.

After the four weeks concluded, interns were assigned to a sales team. The remaining four weeks of the program included intense shadowing and minor support. Team leads engaged each intern and made it a priority to educate them about why they were doing something, the process for doing it, and what the anticipated outcome was to look like. Between the hard and soft skills learned in the first half of the session and the sales skills learned in the latter half, interns were provided with an immense perspective into how to be effective at selling Bloomberg's products and services.

Aside from learning the actual content, immediacy of feedback is the most visible need for Millennial sellers, as they are hungry to apply this new knowledge. Feedback is critical in ensuring that seller actions remain in line with the preferred approach, be it successfully targeting prospects or prioritizing efforts. Managers should minimize the delay in feedback as much as possible because Millennials are used to having information "on-demand." If the training is conducted in a classroom setting, L&D (learning and development) should make sure there are exercises with role-play that allow for immediate feedback. However, the most effective way to train Millennial sellers is by observing them in the field and providing the feedback as immediately as possible.

Recently, David coached a Millennial calling on a strategic opportunity that would have been a net-new win for the company. The rep was well-prepared for the meeting (e.g., company research, reviewing LinkedIn profiles of the meeting participants) but his soft skills needed some attention, specifically his listening and presentation skills. After the sales call, he requested feedback and coaching, in contrast to some of the other sellers we have coached who take more of a passive approach. In the lobby of the prospect's building, right after the meeting, this Millennial seller asked David, "What did you observe and how can I do better?" Though David would have felt more comfortable delivering this feedback in the car, what have we learned about immediacy? Provide the feedback right away, and be sure to follow up to see how the feedback is being applied to make sure they are progressing. Especially important for Millennials, this follow-up technique can be uniformly applied across generations. David told the Millennial seller, "You did a good deal right in that meeting, and I am especially impressed with your level of preparation. I can spend more time on the observations in the future. Can I have your permission to offer some coaching? [This is a key question to gain entry to development.] There were some opportunities to listen closer and get more information. The decision-maker eluded to the decision process multiple times, the time lines, and the main drivers of the project. You did not seek more information at all, and there is much to be learned. We can table the discussion about what else we can work on together until later, but right now we have to focus on identifying key opportunities to dig deeper and learn more. Does that make sense to you?" The Millennial seller was pleased that he was getting real feedback and was eager to keep the coaching dialogue open.

Gen X Sales Professionals Training Tips

Gen Xers typically think, "How is this relevant and useful to me?" In training, Gen X learners often seek relevance and aim to save energy by ignoring the pieces they do not feel directly apply to them or their role. Remember what we learned earlier: Gen X has a need to be independent or to "chart their own course" when learning. Having lived through a deep and painful recession during their prime earning years, Gen X is waiting for the next big growth opportunity. If you were a Gen X sales professional, your world was wildly interrupted in 2008 when the financial planets collided. No matter the level of skill development or preparedness, many sellers questioned their abilities as B2B buying lagged. Gen X, currently in their 40s, are likely experiencing a learning hangover from that experience and have developed a bit of a hard edge. Gen X has endured sales training after sales training to address or fix lagging sales and could tire from the next "flavor of the day." Training should include a fair amount of activities and individual report-backs. As with Baby Boomers, building experiential exercises and activities into training is important. However, unlike their Baby Boomer predecessors, Gen Xers are still looking to prove themselves and itching to "show their stuff." It's a good idea to give Gen X learners opportunities to co-lead training, take the lead on report-backs, and otherwise shine in front of their peers. "Teaching others" is the top way to keep Gen X engaged in learning activities, as they are already primed to take the lead, which in turn boosts their own learning.

We have observed Gen X learners in hundreds of training environments. Our experience is that they rarely excel at "inner thoughts" during training. Rather, the first chance they get to share a difference of opinion, they take it! Recently, David led a workshop packed with more than 100 learners. The session audience was a multigenerational mash-up; the content focused on the skills embedded in a full sales process deployment. During the portion of training focused on "discovery," David had a Gen X participant ask, "This is all great theory, but when will we address the reality of what we deal with trying to position a relatively unknown brand?" He could tell that other generations in the audience felt the back-handed comment a bit crass, though as a fellow Gen Xer, the question did not fluster him a bit. What's more is that all of the other Gen X sellers in the room perked up, as they wanted to see how the trainer would handle the hot potato he was just thrown. David responded, "I am not sure if you asked a question or just made a statement. The workshop is not focused on brand building, but we are currently looking at the process required to better understand the customer. Regardless of brand challenges, it is hard to argue with the theory that understanding the customer could lead to more sales later on in the process. May we all continue?" Thankfully, he allowed him to move on, or it would have turned into a jousting match. This example defines the Gen X learner as they are seeking the short-cut and want to limit the "fluff" as much as possible. They smell "canned" training from a mile away, and unlike their Baby Boomer peers, they do not wait for the first break to pull the trainer aside and communicate any negative observations. They attack in the session, in front of their peers. In the field, the Gen X learner is easy to work with so long as the skills being developed are useful and lead to earning potential. So when training this generation, the material and the person communicating it must get right to the point and immediately engage the audience.

Baby Boomer Sales Professionals Training Tips

Baby Boomers typically think, "I am listening, but prove to me why I should continue?" This is a sales professional with potentially 30+ years of relevant experience and that must be respected. Any training that hopes to snap people into reality or make them change everything is doomed to fail with this audience. Younger generations must resist the urge to brand them as impossible. They are not; they just require us to consider how we can use them to validate the content and earn trust by identifying relevant reasons why making some degree of change is worth the effort.

We can make many correlations to the Gen X learner for the Baby Boomers. They prefer face-to-face training, require feedback, do well with exercises, and want the opportunity to share what life has taught them. The biggest difference is that they will likely pull the trainer aside at a break and ask for the permission to speak up, because they can be more "politically correct." Expect them to take a "wait and see" approach until they smell tried and true methods that can be built on what they have been taught before. Avoid messaging that dictates, "This is the right way and every other way is wrong," and because of this, anticipating incremental change is much more likely than all-out transformation.

David had a classic Baby Boomer experience that helps paint this picture well. He was delivering a leadership program for a client, and two of the sales leaders had many years of experience under their belts. While reviewing the material in advance of an upcoming seller session, leaders were provided with the opportunity to provide feedback. One leader was very quiet and only spoke up when David called on him, but did share his experiences, which was helpful in providing color commentary for the content they were discussing. After the session, this leader approached David offline and told him that he thought the content was rock solid and that the "younger" guys really need the basics in blocking and tackling. Another Baby Boomer in the session asked a question about another method he was very familiar with and quoted the material well. Fortunately, David knew exactly what he was asking for and taught the method he asked about, so David was able to address his question and build trust. He gave David the head nod of approval and was more engaged from that moment on. Regardless of the delivery method, this is what Baby Boomers are looking for: "We are listening, but you have to prove it to me."

Now that we have some idea for how we can be more aware of, and adjust, our approach when training different generations, let's focus on some other ways organizations can hone seller skills.

. . . .

Rotational Programs That Develop Sales Skills

A great way for companies to accelerate the development of selling skills is through compelling rotational programs. These programs provide an opportunity for sellers to experience multiple roles within the organization and develop a broader set of skills in a shorter amount of time than traditional job postings that can last between 12 and 24 months. It sounds like a compelling argument, but our research shows that most companies are not offering what many sellers are seeking: 63 percent of our survey respondents said that their company does not offer a rotational program, though many, specifically Millennials, like to work across departments as they seek to collaborate as a team and find their organizational fit. Mullen Lowe, a Boston-based full-service integrated advertising agency, seemed to echo this conclusion. In an interview, Kristen Cavallo explained, "Given their jungle-gym career trajectories, I believe such a system is definitely a draw for Millennials. This type of flexibility is very appealing to Millennials as they are finding their way into a role they want to settle in to."

Interestingly, as organizations consider a rotational program, they must also consider the types of jobs included and the length of the rotations. Seventy-one percent of our survey respondents thought that if a sales rotation program were offered, the rotations should last 12 months, or less. Millennials felt even more strongly about this short rotation length, with 87 percent of Millennials saying it should be 12 months or less.

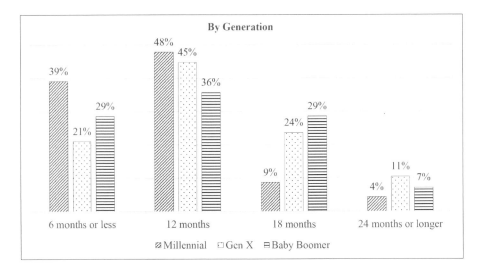

This clearly demonstrates the need for a structured program that moves people along quickly. Through this data, we can see that Millennials have an expectation to learn and acquire skills more quickly than the other generations which, if implemented effectively, can do a lot for employee engagement and retention.

We asked Larry Nettles from PGI about his experience with rotational programs, and he told us about a program at AT&T that involved a rotation of new hires through different roles across a five-year period. The overall objective of the program was to help the new hires build the skills they needed to get to mid-management within five years. Larry told us, "Expectations from the different generations about career paths aren't different; I just find that Millennial expectations are more compressed. Companies have to figure out what type of rotation program would work for them, but we would expect the role rotations to be shorter periods of time so as not to lose the Millennial's interest."

One of the main reasons rotational programs are so effective is that learners are not given a series of "learning shots" that immediately make them more effective. Learning and development take time to become a reality and instantiated into a seller's approach to selling. Moving across roles, and having the opportunity to develop along the way, is a manageable way for people to learn and to begin ingraining important lessons into their daily routine.

A great example we often see involves new sellers starting out by handling smaller accounts and then being promoted to work larger, more strategic customers. This type of a program allows people to master some core skills before they begin to handle customers of greater impact. The game is different with larger accounts, and there are risks in starting people out in these roles. Generational nuances do impact a program of this type. Millennials or starting sales professionals like this structure and have more patience in the program. When a Gen Xer or a Baby Boomer enters this structure, the company has to consider how to handle a person with more experience so they do not flame out before they have the chance to move on to more strategic customers. Let's be clear: this may be life and work experience, and not sales experience. When considering the type of program to establish, consider future needs. Are you currently lacking a leadership pipeline? What about the demand for additional sellers in the next 12, 24, or 36 months? These are just a few of the questions you can ask. Defining a program based on future needs may make more sense given the dynamic way in which business environments shift.

Before we move on and explore the benefits associated with leveraging technology to enable sales skill development, we want to point out the importance of making good on the promises associated with a rotational program. Should the goal of a leadership program be to lead to a more senior title with additional responsibilities, it is imperative that you have a role ready and waiting for these individuals at the completion of the rotation. Not having the promised role available will diminish the value of the program, demotivate those considering the program, and lead to increased turnover. Remember: You have just created a kind of Special Forces leader, seller, or product specialist. The time that's been invested is significant and the value immeasurable; all these things look very good to potential recruiters and corporate suiters alike.

. . . .

Technology Enabling Sales Skill Building

Companies can use many tools to further enable development of sales skills. We often tell sales professionals that life happens at two speeds: practice speed and game speed. You have to practice well enough at close to game speed so that you may respond more favorably when the real pressure is on. This is true in sports, and it certainly applies to sales (and especially public speaking). Because practicing on customers is never suggested, we are left with looking for ways to either witness real customer situations or practice them, via role-play, whenever possible. In David's early days of inside sales, calls would be recorded so that sales managers could analyze how they handled an opportunity. This was primitive, but it did serve well in helping people to hear game speed interactions and analyze their own skills. Today, we can still record a call but recording an outside sale is a bit trickier.

Technology offered by many companies today allows sales enablement teams to program or engineer sales interactions in a fashion similar to a cartoon. It may sound odd, but the finished product is very professional. As long as the scripts are well-written, people can really learn from these tools. The learner can either watch the whole interaction or choose what the seller asks in order to see how the customer responds. Imagine a cartoon-based sales chess game that allows sellers to proactively experiment in a safe learning environment.

Some learning and development firms offer pre-built content that can be deployed, but we strongly suggest a few things. One, consider your audience. More experienced sellers will likely have a negative reaction to these types of learning modules and may see them as a cheap way to avoid developing skills or creating and executing face-to-face sessions. Two, take the time to customize these tools to fit your sales model and business language. Generic modules are often not taken that seriously. Three, use these tools to supplement other things you are doing to build skills. This medium should be additive to a robust platform of building sales skills. Four, if you have people starting their sales careers, or seeking to engage

Millennials, this medium may be smart to use, as they are comfortable with both distance learning and technology.

Getting Started

When it comes to tailoring training and development efforts based on generations, one of the best practices we've observed is implementing a training advisory board composed of people from each generation represented in the sales force. The training advisory board would make decisions on the training content covered, the best content design, and content delivery channel with the goal of meeting the needs of the multigenerational sales team.

We recently delivered a pilot workshop for a client who allowed their sales organization to validate the content topics, gain specific customization feedback, and test the session with a select group of sales reps. During the pilot session, there was a strong mix of generations. We discussed the needs of each type of learner so that we could customize the workshop based on the generational mix. In the end, the company decided that for training outside sellers, the best delivery channel would be one-on-one in-the-field training, which would be reinforced by team meetings and individual leader-driven modules as-needed. They decided not to deploy online courses or classroom sessions in this case. The company made a great decision based on the generational mix of its sales team because, although they did have a mix of people represented, the team had a high percentage of experienced sellers. Experienced sellers will react better and learn faster from training that is more hands-on. The decision to not use online courses was the right one for a couple of reasons: first, this is the least preferred method of learning across the generations, and second, more experienced sellers will be much less engaged and interested in learning from online modules. Although it may have been faster and cost-effective, the desired outcomes would have been less than expected.

In summary, there are many ways that companies can approach the development of sales skills, but those who get training right spend extra time up-front considering the generational mix of their audience and tailoring the training approach accordingly.

Even the best training and development programs can fail without the proper management and oversight. In the next chapter, we will look at important management skills and leadership styles that should be leveraged in order to reinforce many of the concepts introduced in this chapter.

7

Sales Coaching and Performance Management

"Serving my generation with excellence will mean, in turn, my generation can lead with excellence."

—Onyi Anyado, entrepreneur and leadership speaker (1976–)

If you have ever spent a day of your life as a sales leader, you know that managing sales professionals with different personalities, motivators, and development areas is hard enough, but then layer in the complexity of a multigenerational team, and the differences in needs and perspectives of the sellers are even further magnified.

For example, David has had the pleasure of leading sales teams and sales leaders more than a few times. It comes with days that are fun, days that are insane, and days that make you want to pull your own teeth out. At one point in his career, David managed a team of three sales leaders and 20 sales professionals. The sales leaders were all Baby Boomers, and the rest of the sales team was a mix of Baby Boomers and Gen Xers. The sales team had marketing resources, mostly Millennials, to help drive pre- and post-sales support, which made sense given many of the customers were also of the same generation. This generational mix caused issues with respect to sales coaching, and performance management was a real mess for a variety of reasons. Often David conducted ride-alongs with a specific seller who was quite a few years older. David was in his early 40s, the seller in his mid-50s. During the first ride-along, the sales rep looked right at David and asked, "What can I expect to learn from you, junior?" Needless to say, this was a rough start for their working relationship. David needed to quickly locate something—anything—that would allow him to add credibility to his leadership title. Quickly during the ride-along, he noticed a flaw in the seller's approach that was not helping his cause: his discovery questions sounded like trial closes, which added too much pressure to the meeting. The decision-maker was clearly put off the seller's approach and actually called him out for being overly "salesy." The seller still missed the cues.

After the meeting, David said, "Can junior have permission to share a few observations?" His question broke the ice and made them both chuckle. First, David shared a list of all of the stuff the seller did well, and the list was long. He then pointed out all of the exact moments when the decision-maker became uncomfortable with the pressure created by the invasive discovery questions that all sounded like, "If we do x, would you do y?" *Quid pro quo*–style questions. David referred to the moments when the decision-maker used the term *salesy*, and by that point in the coaching conversation, he had his attention. In the end, the seller took David's feedback well and thanked him for noticing the subtle things that were causing his sales to go awry. Together they crafted a few strategies to approach his next meeting, which showed him that David was squarely on his side. Through this experience, David learned that, though coaching and performance improvement are tricky on their own, the sales rep's perception of David's youth at the time only made it more challenging.

According to a recent Careerbuilder.com survey, 69 percent of workers 55 and older actually report to a younger manager.[1] This is directionally consistent with the data in our Generational Selling Survey as well. Our survey data shows that Gen Xers are the predominate population of direct managers for the population we surveyed: 57 percent of Baby Boomer sales professionals report to Gen X managers, 60 percent of Gen X sales professionals report to Gen X managers, and 52 percent of Millennial sales professionals are reporting to Gen X managers.

	Baby Boomer (Manager)	Gen X (Manager)	Millennial (Manager)
Baby Boomer	39%	57%	4%
Gen X	40%	60%	-
Millennial	18%	52%	30%
All	33%	57%	10%

Simply put, we have a large percentage of Gen X sales leaders leading multigenerational teams. Not only are many of these jobs high pressure, but many sales managers are also trying to solve for the generational puzzle with little knowledge or training on what to do.

It's important to evaluate the composition of your sales team and determine what coaching or performance management tactics may need to be adjusted in light of a seller's generation. You have learned a great deal already in this book, and we can confidently tell you that Generational Flexibility will be one of your go-to tools when it comes to coaching and performance management. This is a two-way street, so sales managers and sellers should both tune in closely to this chapter to discover new ideas on ways to not only communicate more effectively, but to also give and receive coaching and performance feedback.

The Concept of Time

One of the first things successful managers must learn is how best to identify and support the needs of their direct reports while balancing the expectations placed upon them by their own leadership team. Most managers would love the opportunity to be out in the field supporting sellers and helping to provide the coaching necessary to elevate performance. When we think about what makes a good manager, words like *mentor* and *coach* ring true, though the reality requires them to do, and be, so much more. Daily demands, internal issue resolution, upstream management, and unhappy customers are just some of the scenarios that seem to plop onto the plates of most, if not all, sales leaders.

Sales leaders grapple with how to determine how much time to spend coaching their sales team versus all of the other important strategic activities. Unfortunately, this is not a "one size fits all" approach. Managers struggle with various issues, from managing sellers from multiple generations to not having the time to manage at all, as they spend the majority of their time tracking down performance reports or trying to engage employees remotely. Companies will often put forth a formal performance management cadence but will fall far short of providing sufficient guidance for coaching. Dictating a formal performance management approach is better than no approach at all, but the fact of the matter is that managing individuals will look very different from person to person. Without a formal approach, managers tend to manage others the way they prefer to be managed themselves.

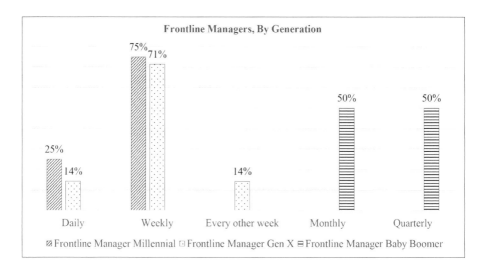

This point was made supported by our survey, which cited 100 percent of Millennial managers indicating that they provide coaching daily or weekly. This is in stark contrast to Baby Boomer managers, 100 percent of whom said that they provide coaching on a monthly or quarterly basis. This could be correlated with the type of sales teams that each manage. Inside sales teams require much more frequent coaching and feedback, with everyone typically centrally located and sales cycles that allow for coaching interactions on a daily basis. Field sales teams are typically dispersed, requiring the manager to travel to spend quality coaching time with each seller, a much more infrequent proposition.

When contemplating how to effectively divide up the day, managers should not assume that age, experience, or even their own desired frequency for feedback constitute the level of attention a seller might desire. For example, one might think that experienced Baby Boomer sellers need less coaching than Millennial sellers. It is a common assumption perpetuated by the perception that Baby Boomers have seen and done it all, and that Millennials may require more time, attention, and guidance. This is a perfect example for how generational awareness, or a lack thereof, can cloud judgment. Before we address the possible time demands of the Millennial generation, let's explore the negative implications associated with leaving even the most tenured sellers to weather the sales process with little to no support.

A recent client we worked with in the software industry was faced with putting a monthly sales management cadence in place for a team that calls on high-value strategic accounts, mostly large global banks. The team was primarily made up of Baby Boomer sellers with decades of experience. To make matters worse, the Gen X managers received a fair amount of pushback as sellers voiced the seemingly obvious fact that "nothing really changes in these accounts week over week." Leadership understood their concerns, but the needs of the business were driving the program. The company needed more visibility into opportunities within a specific group of strategic clients, as these accounts represented 53 percent of revenues. Even if opportunities weren't closing, it was important to review leading indicators, such as prospecting activity and customer engagement, to ensure that the right activities were being executed in support of a robust pipeline.

During these meetings, managers were expected to coach sellers on ways to positively influence the progression of the opportunity through the sales pipeline, and to ensure that the right relationships were being developed to provide long-term value for both the company and their customers. By clearly communicating the motivating factors, the company was able to lessen pushback by being open and transparent. This gave way to a more frequent coaching cadence and an open and informal dialogue between Baby Boomer sellers and Gen X managers. Leaders gained immediate visibility into the brightest opportunities, were able to put the right focus on the right deals, and assisted sellers in tweaking their approach. Through this process, leadership was able to support certain deals and quickly uncovered several internal operational issues that were inhibiting the progression of these more strategic opportunities. Simple tweaks to the sales approach and modifications to internal RFP processes allowed this group of Baby Boomer sellers to become exponentially more efficient.

How a company—and manager, for that matter—positions coaching can make or break adoption, especially if the desired behavior is counter to an assumed generational preference. In this case, skeptical Baby Boomers soon became receptive to the heightened focus, as there was real value created for the company, sellers, and their clients. Assuming that even the most experienced Baby Boomer sellers do not need regular coaching is a big miss. It's often these experienced sellers who have the wherewithal to identify creative solutions that may be hindering success; just be sure to be transparent and delineate the value to be gained for all parties.

Now that we understand the value of coaching for even the most experienced sellers, let us turn our attention back to the Millennial dilemma. A friend of our firm, and successful sales manager, confirmed that, though her newer Millennial sellers required more attention, recognition, coaching, and feedback, she did not attribute this to being stereotypically "needy." She contributed her observations to their relative insecurity due to their level of inexperience: "They are simply seeking validation that they are on the right track." A more tenured seller does not typically have the same insecurities. This sales manager told us, "When I look at the situation [that way] it reverses my thinking and shifts any annoyance to compassion." She also shared, "If you develop a mindset that allows you to seek to understand what it is like to enter a role, or company, where you are surrounded by people with decades of experience, you will feel differently." What's even more important to recognize is that this generation doesn't want their hand held, but they are seeking very pointed, yet constructive, feedback. Understanding when and how to provide that feedback will be critical to your success as a coach.

We interviewed Steve Richard and David Stillman from a company called Vorsight, which provides outsourced appointment setting, training, and consulting services to sales organizations. The company employs a large Millennial sales force whose primary role is to work on behalf of their clients to schedule sales interactions with prospects. Steve and David believe that for their Millennial sellers, "iterative learning is key" and that managers should "give feedback in bite-sized chunks, and consistently apply a rhythm and routine to their informal feedback." Steve and David strongly believe that these conversations can, and should, happen in a variety of formats: in the hallway, in one-on-ones, and after job shadowing. Also understanding that many companies have matrixed organizational structures, managers should be comfortable with, and even encourage, multiple layers of people in different roles giving feedback to their sellers. If a manager has a seller who craves feedback, the manager should proactively seek out other leaders, mentors, or peers to provide feedback to these eager sellers. Great managers will leverage their internal networks as a coaching amplifier.

David and Steve both advise that it is important to highlight incremental improvements for Millennial sellers. "If Millennials don't see the immediate impact from the feedback or change they make, they will be quick to cut off the feedback channel." Because of this risk, whenever a manager can help Millennial sellers arrive at a coaching moment on their own, it can be much more impactful than telling a Millennial what to do differently. What is the adaptation? More coaching, smaller coaching moments, and everyone can be a coach.

When establishing your cadence, we recommend you trust and verify. Trust shows inherent respect for those on your team, and a well-manageable cadence allows you to ascertain who on the team needs help and how to scale your efforts across the team. Though a formal cadence sets expectations for what the team can expect by way of team meetings, one-on-ones, ride-alongs, opportunity reviews, and win-loss analyses, unplanned and informal chats can be leveraged to keep younger generations engaged. Should a seller require less time, shift your attention to team members who require more time. Leverage experienced sellers, with behaviors you would like others to emulate, to assist you in providing feedback. Empower experienced sellers by engaging them as peer mentors and be sure to aggregate best practices and share them when it is appropriate.

The Type of Leadership and Coaching Sellers Demand

Coaching, in its simplest form, is an approach that typically revolves around a more experienced and knowledgeable individual supporting or guiding a lesser experienced learner. The reality is, experience alone is necessary, but not sufficient to make an effective coach. In many scenarios, the lesser experienced generation is coaching an older generation with more experience. Let's explore this concept further by defining the impact leadership styles have on a coach's ability to be effective.

To be an effective coach, you need only give that which you expect to receive: respect. This is the challenge that many sales leaders struggle to define as it relates to managing and coaching the performance of a multi-generational sales team. If respect is the end game, a coach must be astutely aware of their specific leadership style. The way in which they lead their teams has an immediate and lasting impact on the individual's willingness to heed the advice of their coach.

Three of the most discussed leadership styles include authoritarian, democratic, and laissez-faire (hands-off). Each with a unique blend of motivations and desired outcomes, we argue that a single approach applied to unique team members is a mistake. Instead, being aware for when and how to leverage certain leadership styles can provide a benefit as you seek to secure the respect that precedes valuable coaching. Note that there are many well-established coaching models, and we often work with clients who have trained their teams on programs such as Situational Leadership II from the Ken Blanchard Companies or programs from the Center for Creative Leadership.

Imagine a continuum. On the left hand side, you have democratic; on the right, laissez-faire. Let's look at the laissez-faire style first. At times discounted as a lazy way to lead, this style can result in a lack of control, increasing costs, and poor performance. In the context of a sales environment, however, this approach may be exactly what's required to allow highly qualified Baby Boomer sellers to perform uninhibited. These experienced sellers don't need additional motivation, and apart from their clearly articulated sales goals, do not require guidance or supervision in most cases.

Contrast this with the democratic, or participatory, leadership style, which provides the collaboration required to keep Millennials engaged. By offering guidance, but allowing team members to weigh in, democratic leaders boost employee morale and level of creativity, as well as perpetuate the notion that their opinions do matter.

You might be thinking, "Well, where does Gen X fit?" It would be easy to characterize Gen Xers as a wooden peg on the sliding continuum. Although it is quite possible that observable behavior will dictate where on the continuum they fall, we suggest employing a transformational leadership style given the impact this generation has on bringing teams together and their pending roles as future leaders. Transformational leaders are committed to not only hitting their sales targets but in helping team members realize their professional potential.

As referenced in a recent article by Verywell.com, "Research has revealed that this style of leadership resulted in higher performance and improved group satisfaction than other leadership styles. One study also found that transformation leadership led to improved well-being among group members."[2]

Employing our "trust and verify" motto, leadership styles should err on the side of trust.

Unfortunately, circumstances may arise that require the leader to change tactics (for instance, when a Baby Boomer seller needs a bit of motivation and direction or a Millennial begins tracking poorly against their plan). As these scenarios arise, leaders can employ a more autocratic approach most often utilized when employees require closer supervision. If utilized incorrectly, this approach can be viewed as bossy or dictatorial, though helping to define what is required, when it's required, and how it should be done will provide the guidance required to get sellers back on track. There are times when the right approach becomes highly directive in nature so that sellers are reminded of expectations and requirements.

Once you command respect, only then will your feedback and constructive criticisms be taken to heart. Moving past how to engage an individual team member, it's also important to consider where to engage that individual. Let us now turn our attention to the various formats that can be more or less effective based upon a seller's generation. When we asked responders about the format of coaching sales managers and sellers felt was most effective (1 is most effective and 5 is least effective), we found that they preferred more personalized coaching, like one-on-one coaching or "in-the-field" coaching, over less scalable options like "peer-to peer" or "group" coaching.

Ordering of Coaching Preferences

(1=Most Preferred; 5=Least Preferred)

	All
1.	One-on-One Coaching
2.	Curbside "In the Field" Coaching
3.	Peer-to-Peer Coaching
4.	Group Coaching
5.	No Coaching

This is not surprising and actually validates an age-old theory: praise in public and discipline in private. Most of us prefer to deal with performance improvement one-on-one. Next, we looked at the data by generation, and the ordering of coaching method effectiveness was also aligned. People of all generations want personalized attention from a sales leader or peer.

Ordering of Coaching Preferences

(1=Most Preferred; 5=Least Preferred)

	Millennial	Gen	Baby Boomer
1.	One-on-One Coaching	One-on-One Coaching	One-on-One Coaching
2.	Curbside "In the Field" Coaching	Curbside "In the Field" Coaching	Peer-to-Peer Coaching
3.	Peer-to-Peer Coaching	Peer-to-Peer Coaching	Group Coaching
4.	Group Coaching	Group Coaching	Curbside "In the Field" Coaching
5.	No Coaching	No Coaching	No Coaching

The DNA of Successful Managers

Several research studies in the past decade have confirmed that the most common reason that employees leave a company is due to their immediate supervisor.[3] In sales, this equally applies and also contributes to the second most common reason, which is poor sales performance. We talked with Ewelina Wojnowska, a high-performing national account executive for CareerBuilder, about the qualities she thinks are most important in a great sales manager. She told us "the person that you report to (as a seller) is extremely important. I think the most important quality for a manager is that he or she has your back. In sales, it's easy to feel like you are at the bottom of the totem pole because of the different layers of leadership (internally and within the customer organization) making decisions. Having a manager who has your back by helping you figure out why a customer meeting got cancelled, or navigating the customer organization, etc., is critical. My manager is very supportive and helps me think outside the box." The data from our survey backs the theory that a supportive sales manager is the top quality that sellers prefer.

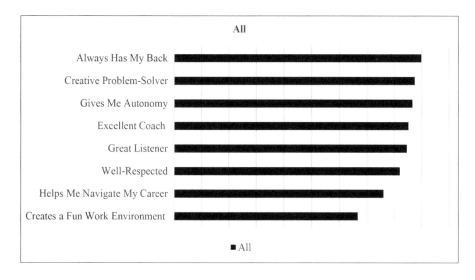

Not surprisingly, however, when you look at the data broken out by generation, you start to notice some nuances. For example, overall Millennial sellers ranked "excellent coach" as their top manager quality and Baby Boomer sellers ranked "creative problem solver" as their top manager quality.

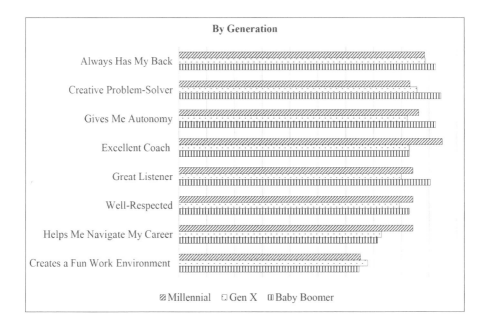

This research demonstrates how generational nuances affect the perception of a strong sales manager. For example, a "creative problem solver" is likely more valuable to a Baby Boomer because they can get most of the job done on their own and really only need a strong manager for when a challenging problem arises.

When we saw this data, we immediately thought of a seller David had managed who fit this bill. Jim was a Baby Boomer who never missed a quota but always seemed to get himself into a pickle over relationships, selling additional solutions, and managing the politics of his accounts. He routinely drove the business forward, and when David saw his phone signal a call from him, he knew he was going to get a 45-minute story before he would ask him for his thoughts; in the last five minutes of the conversation, he ultimately wanted advice on how he could solve the problem. Millennials, on the other hand, see other qualities as more valuable. They are looking for a great coach and someone who helps them navigate their career. This makes sense because they have less experience, want more coaching, and desire feedback to help propel their career forward.

Another common characteristic of great sales leaders is the ability to "create a fun work environment." All three generations value a fun work environment relatively the same, with Gen X preferring it a little more. We firmly believe that people do not look in the mirror each morning and say, "I hope today is miserable and boring." Sales often attracts fun people with big personalities. It is important to remember that leaders should recognize the importance of the "fun factor." Making budgets and goals is critical, but some fun along the way is absolutely acceptable and will aid in strengthening the bond among team members. One of our colleagues previously worked for a large global consulting and training organization. There was a sales team for middle markets that missed their goal quarter after quarter. One particularly bad day when they had lost several deals, she invited her team into her office, turned on Taylor Swift's song "Shake It Off," and for a solid 10 minutes, they danced away their sorrows. Fast-forward a year, and they are the only program hitting goal!

· ·

Delivering Feedback

One of the most powerful forms of communication is feedback. Our survey data supports the idea that informal settings for receiving feedback are becoming more and more popular, with "in person—formal setting" coming in at a very close second (1 is most preferred and 5 is least preferred).

Ordering of Feedback Preferences

(1=Most Preferred; 5=Least Preferred)

	All
1.	In Person—Informal Setting (e.g. over lunch, coffee, etc.)
2.	In Person—Formal Setting (e.g. in the office)
3.	In the field (e.g. after a client meeting wraps)
4.	Over email
5.	Over video recorded feedback

The rising popularity of informal feedback settings is causing sales organizations to rethink the way that they manage performance. Take a company called Wunderman, who employs a large Millennial workforce. Wunderman created "YouTime," a system that encourages managers and employees to discuss goals and accomplishments in informal settings like a manicure or even a dance class, supplementing more regularly structured check-ins and reviews. "The older structures almost made people feel bad if they wanted to discuss raises and promotion," said Seth Solomons, CEO of North America at Wunderman. "We are unlearning a lot of those bad habits. 'YouTime' is an open space for them to go ahead and advocate for themselves."[4] Creating an open forum like YouTime is a perfect example of how companies with multigenerational sales teams can tweak, or add to, a more formal company-wide performance management process.

We often see companies encourage one-on-one time between sellers and managers, but they rarely suggest what the setting should be for these feedback sessions. David had the pleasure of being managed by a man named Larry Walker, who served in the U.S. Airforce and then went on to lead countless sales teams. Larry passed away in 2002 and is dearly missed by everyone he touched. David spent more than 10 years of his career working for Larry, who said, "You will always know exactly where you stand with me, your performance, what you excel at and where you can improve if you are on my team." The setting did not matter, as Larry had the unique ability to reach people, be it within a formal post–sales call coaching session or informal lunches and dinners with too many cock-tails and an immeasurable amount of laughter. What Larry was able to exude so effortlessly is an approach leaders should seek to emulate. His ability to set clear expectations and perpetuate open lines of communi-cation broke down barriers. Formal or informal settings aside, when you respect those who provide you with feedback and direction, the value is mutually realized. Many sales teams (and workers in other functional areas) are increasingly working from home or from remote offices, and are not co-located with their sales manager. Sales leaders must learn from the research and take to heart that some forms of feedback, though ef-ficient, are less desirable to sellers of certain generations. We know this sounds like common sense, but relying solely on email is not an efficient avenue for providing coaching and feedback, especially when there is a skill gap that requires practice. It's bad enough that it is now acceptable to break up with people over text, so do whatever is possible to not manage the work relationship over email.

Minimizing Turnover

There are some things that eat time and cause blurry-eyed frustration for sales managers, and turnover is one of them. Let's look at turnover driv-ers, by generation. Not surprisingly, sellers from all generations ranked "offered a better compensation package" as their top turnover driver. "Bad leadership" fell among the top four drivers for all three generations as well. Let's consider these two "table stakes" when it comes to driving high sales employee engagement.

Millennials	Gen X	Baby Boomers
Offered a better compensation package	Offered a better compensation package	Offered a better compensation package
No opportunities to get promoted	No opportunities to get promoted	Bad leadership
Lack of flexibility (e.g. time, location, etc.)	Bad leadership	Offered a better title
Bad Leadership	Offered a better title	Poor reputation of the company
Boring work culture	Not challenged by current role	No opportunities to get promoted
Not challenged by current role	Lack of flexibility (e.g. time, location, etc.)	Lack of flexibility (e.g. time, location, etc.)
Offered a better title	Poor reputation of the company	Not challenged by current role
Limited training/ development opportunities	Limited training/ development opportunities	Little collaboration across team
Little collaboration across team	Little collaboration across team	Limited training/ development opportunities
Poor reputation of the company	Boring work culture	Boring work culture

Interesting, however, was that Millennials ranked "lack of flexibility" their third driver for Millennial turnover; this driver was ranked sixth for both Gen Xers and Baby Boomers. If a company is planning to, or already has, a large cohort of Millennials, this is worth taking notice. Millennials may desire a more open dialogue about work/life balance, the ability to work from home, or the option to work flexible hours for one reason or another. But, some leaders, depending on their generation, may want sellers to prove their worth before they trust that their sellers can perform outside of typical working hours or arrangements.

Also interesting was that Baby Boomers ranked "poor reputation of the company" fourth as a turnover driver, whereas Gen Xers ranked it seventh and Millennials ranked it last. Again, Baby Boomers are trust-based people and therefore the reputation of the company is extremely important. Trust is embedded in their sales DNA and if the company does not fit the mold, they will leave in many cases. On the other hand, Millennials are more open to taking risks, even if the company is not yet well-established or in start-up mode, because of where they are in their careers.

· · · · · · ·

These past several chapters have focused on how sales organizations must adapt to effectively leverage multigenerational talent. In the final two chapters, we will speak directly to sellers (Chapter 8) and sales managers (Chapter 9) to provide those of you in these roles with specific advice on how to put the ideas from this book into practice.

8 A Message to Sellers

"The most aggravating thing about the younger generation is that I no longer belong to it."

—Albert Einstein, German-born theoretical physicist (1879–1955)

For those of you who are in sales and responsible for hitting a number, explicit or otherwise, this chapter is for you. Your job is not always easy. Changing seller and buyer dynamics force you to adapt as competition increases, availability to information becomes more overwhelming and the power seems to continue to shift from seller to buyer. Across industries and selling models, one thing that remains consistent for organizations is that it is difficult to find talented sellers, and developing and engaging them is even harder.

We would like you to meet our friend Brian, a Gen X sales rep in Brooklyn, New York, who has had an amazing sales career. David and Brian worked very closely together for almost a decade, so David knows that Brian is the type of guy who is always on the stage at the awards banquet and never misses a President's Club trip. However, one year in particular, Brian ran up against some insurmountable obstacles, caus-ing him to lose a few very strategic accounts. This client turnover caused Brian to fall short of the "Club" qualification. David remembers Brian saying, "You know I will make the Club next year without the 'whale' accounts. I will just have to work harder to sell more small accounts. I believe that recovering from a bad year is a mark of success, and I glad-ly accept the challenge. I will do whatever I have to do, even if it means prospecting like I did when I first started in sales. Just watch me." The next year, not only did Brian qualify for the President's Club trip, he also earned Sales Rep of the Year.

Great sellers are special and should be considered valuable assets within a sales organization. Often sales organizations are considered cost centers, but what many of these organizations don't understand is that it is the individual selling the product or service who must be able to cut through the over commoditization that occurs in most selling scenarios. We have spent most of our careers, and a large part of the research effort for this book, focusing on the characteristics of top performing sales pro-fessionals.[1] So, this content is especially for you.

In this chapter, we focus on providing advice and lessons learned from high-performing sales professionals with a variety of backgrounds and experiences to help you, as the seller, find success (or higher levels of success). We explore what sellers, regardless of their level of experience, should consider and then speak specifically to new sellers, as well as to sellers who are more tenured. We do this because we strongly believe that there are certain elements, call them skills or abilities, that every seller should possess—regardless of their level of experience. All sellers must practice these elements in order to secure long-term success in sales. Our goal is that by the end of this chapter, no matter what your current situa-tion is as a seller, you will learn something that you can put into practice immediately that will help improve your performance.

Advice for All Sellers

As mentioned, there are certain elements that every seller should possess regardless of experience. The added complexity of mixing sellers, sales leaders, and customers from a variety of generations makes these elements even more important. Here are a few recommendations for all sellers to abide by, regardless of years of experience or generation.

Continue to Strengthen Your Communications Skills

Whether you are a Millennial, Gen Xer, or Baby Boomer, strong communication skills, with both internal partners and customers, are critical to your success. Communication styles and channels change rapidly, requiring sellers to keep abreast of the new trends that may impact the way they work. Chris Dessi, our go-to social selling expert, suggested to us that sellers "use applications to hone their communication skills." One in particular, known as the Hemingway App, allows sellers to input proposed text in order to gain a sense for how complex the sentence structure might be, along with feedback for how to streamline said text. The app will literally highlight the words and phrases that should be reconsidered for those trying to accomplish bold and succinct communications. Whether seeking out the most eye-catching subject line or determining how to make your message more consumable, there are a slew of apps available to help guide sellers looking to become more effective. Take advantage of these tools, many of which are free, as you seek to increase your level of selling proficiency.

Another key takeaway when considering how best to communicate is understanding the impact and value of curating your own opinion. Let us assume that your company just launched a press release that communicates a new product or service. Many sellers will likely consider bringing this up at their next meeting, though most tend to forget. Others will decide to leverage social media as an avenue by which this news may be immediately shared. Unfortunately, even these sellers often miss the mark when they end up simply sharing the content without so much as an opinion. What's the result? Minimal views, no engagement, and a depressing number of "likes." Have you ever seen a press release? They aren't exactly eye-catching.

Great sellers recognize the potential that a new product or service might have on piquing consumer curiosity and providing them with a valuable opportunity to get their foot in the door. The seller thinks, *"This information is important and I need to distribute it."* By avoiding a network-wide blast, a strategic, well-intentioned, and relevant message can be curated for specific prospects and customers. Customizing this content so that it resonates with the end decision-maker allows the seller to communicate value, and adding their opinion only helps to elevate the level of sincerity felt by the recipient of the content.

Chris explained, "Communicating on social media requires a distinct 'voice' or 'presence,' which is a new skill that requires sellers to invest time and attention in finding the right content and targeting that content for the right decision-maker." Knowing the features and benefits of a product or service is great, but if you cannot communicate those benefits effectively, in a way that matches or compliments a colleague or customer's communication style, your success will be limited.

Build Your Gravitas

Our friend and business partner Mo Bunnell introduced us to the concept of gravitas, which he defines as "substance or depth of personality."[2] There comes a point in all sellers' careers where "fake it until you make it" is no longer an option, which these days is immediately (except for those fortunate enough to land a sales role selling a "hot" product; think software and technology during the dotcom era). Truly successful sellers have both the deep expertise in their respective fields and the confidence to carry a conversation with high-level decision-makers. Often this ability results from a clear understanding of the customers' business aligned with the potential value the firm's products and solutions can deliver. By employing an outside-in and an inside-out approach for strategizing how best to deliver value, sellers are able to define what is most important to the buyer on both a professional and often a personal level. What aspirations does the buyer's firm hold? What are the client's needs and what attributes might be motivating my specific decision-maker? All of these insights are then aligned to the seller's offering.

Great sellers display a substantial desire to learn, submerge themselves in their respective industries, and never miss an opportunity to continue to grow as a professional. As a result, clients love to meet with these sellers because their broader knowledge often fuels a great dialogue and the client always walks away from the conversation having learned something new.

Gravitas also provides you, the seller, with an ability to differentiate yourself with regard to how you sell, not just what you are selling. The famed researcher and author Neil Rackham has offered an excellent example of true consultative selling, which we heard from him when he spoke at a sales conference several years ago: after a customer discussion has concluded, the customer turns to you, the seller, and says that even if they do not purchase your product or service, the conversation has been so valuable and insightful that they would be willing to write you a check for your time. Many sales training programs offer techniques to build your messaging and ability to bring insights to a customer, but fundamentally you, the seller, must develop your own expertise and gravitas, some of which comes with experience as you progress through your selling career.

Be an Agent for Change

If your firm does not take generational differences seriously, then you should take it upon yourself to initiate the changes that will undoubtedly improve outcomes for your internal team and customers. Ask that generational nuances, within reason, be considered during team meetings, in one-on-ones, in training, and when planning for customer interactions. For example, as you think about the make-up of your sales team, ask your sales manager, "Given the generational mix of our team, is a conference call the best way to have our team meeting this month?" As you consider how to strengthen the relationship with an at-risk customer, ask, "Do we have the right people, from a generational perspective, engaged from our team to build this relationship?" These are all questions that will begin the right dialogue about generational obstacles in sales and all generations can benefit from these conversations.

Focus on Pre-Call Planning and Preparation

There is no substitute for being well-prepared for a sales meeting. As we've discussed in the previous chapters, and specifically in Chapter 3, you should weave in the generational considerations to your pre-call planning. Whenever possible, think in advance about the customers and buyers in an upcoming meeting and how you can best prepare for different communication and learning preferences and adjust your style. Consider creating a team of trusted sellers that represents each generation as you seek to more effectively prepare for client meetings. This will allow you the opportunity to practice the content and different delivery techniques in order to mitigate potential generational flare-ups in key meetings. Your generationally diverse peer group can give you feedback that helps you avoid missteps.

Advice for New Sellers

There is an assumption that all new sellers are Millennials. However, knowing anyone can make a career change and find themselves in a sales role, we believe there are ideas that new sellers of all generations should adopt in order to be successful. Even if your long-term career plans do not involve sales, most tenured professionals have some sort of "sales" component to their leadership role. Think about a partner at a law, consulting, or investment firm: these roles all involve selling in some way or another. Even in departments like IT, product development, and marketing, leaders must often sell their ideas to their internal customers. The reality is that whether you plan to have a long-term career in sales, or if you are just using it as a jumping-off point, the skills you learn as a seller will serve you well.

There are many advantages to being a new seller, especially a new Millennial seller, in today's work environment. Millions of Millennials enter the workforce every day. Some will choose sales, and in other cases sales will choose them. (Welcome, geologists, to the profession of sales!) Because of the current mix of generations in the workforce, it is more important than ever to be aware of generational perceptions and equipped with as many tools as possible to overcome unavoidable obstacles. Let's review some of the advantages of being "new" to sales.

Place in Life

Earlier in the book, we introduced the concept of "place in life." There is a statistically higher chance that a new Millennial seller will have less responsibility outside of the office (children, family, etc.). Because of this, new sellers may have the ability to work longer hours and travel more than others, which gives them more chances to gain experience. We have spoken to numerous sellers across many companies who are in this exact situation, and they validate the theory by saying, "I can live the job right now," "I do not have competing responsibilities outside of work, so entertaining clients in the evening is fine with me," and "I am always plugged into technology, so responding to emails in the evening does not concern me." New sellers should capitalize on this and use this time to gain experience and fill the mental bank account—literally. Examples include taking extra time to spend with more experienced sellers and, when possible, observing these sellers in action. New sellers should also spend additional time learning about their customers' industries, and key business drivers and pressures facing their customers (which will help to build their gravitas, as outlined above).

Understanding of Technology

New sellers, especially Millennials, tend to have a strong understanding of technology. There are few technology platforms that a sales organization could choose to implement that you will not be able to figure out quickly and be expert at using within weeks. Most new sellers have grown up with technology and have made it part of their life from the moment they could swipe a screen. A recent client of Symmetrics Group validated this idea when they deployed an iPad-enabled sales tool (CRM) that all sellers use in the field for customer records and intelligence. Leveraging technology as part of the flow in everyday interactions—even at work—is becoming more and more popular. This adjustment will likely be easier for new sellers who have grown up with technology compared to more experienced sellers, who did not. New sellers should leverage all of the sales enablement tools offered by their company along with external tools such as LinkedIn. Although this advice also applies to experienced sellers, new sellers should use these tools as much as possible to shrink their learning curve.

Clean Slate for Learning

New sellers do not have to unlearn bad sales habits that have been built up over a decade or two. Sales leaders will often describe more tenured sellers as sometimes having to unlearn old habits and new sellers as more of a clean slate. The fact is that a new seller may have a few bad habits, but less to unravel. They will let go of what they have previously learned much easier than others and are often very vocal in classroom-based settings and sales team meetings. More often than not, they are sitting in the front row, asking lots of questions, engaging in the exercises, and looking unimpressed at the experienced sellers who openly challenge the content, as they see it as getting in the way of their learning. Less experience can make you more of an open book.

Understanding that new sellers have a built-in runway for learning, here are a few tips to increase the speed going down that runway:

- **Be patient.** Remember that becoming good at anything takes time. As we highlighted in Chapter 6, a majority of sales managers and leaders say it can take anywhere from four to 12 months to become an effective seller. This timeline might seem really long to those starting a career in sales. You may learn facts about your products and services quickly, but the soft skills (communication, presenting, handling objections, negotiating, closing) take time to master, and a year (or several) may not even be enough. For both of us authors, it has taken years to develop solid selling skills, and we are both still learning new things that will increase our abilities and results. Additionally, you may be selling against more tenured sellers who have experience and much deeper relationships with prospects and customers. It will be more difficult for you to unhook relationships that have been in place for a long time, and even in the absence of a relationship, more experienced sellers know how to work their networks to win references you do not yet have. You will have to win on competence, great follow-up, knowing what your customers want, and identifying new ways to relate to buyers. Remember that sales is a numbers game. Take comfort in the fact that in the beginning you may have to work hard to build your portfolio, but with each interaction, you have the opportunity to further refine your knowledge, skills, and abilities.

- **Seek out a mentor.** There are people in addition to your immediate manager, both within and outside your organization, who can teach you the ropes and accelerate your success. Seek out individuals you respect because of their demonstrated knowledge or success in their field and ask them if they would be open to scheduling regular coaching time to give you advice or feedback on customer interactions. A great mentor will give you a safe sounding board and a different—less biased— perspective than your direct sales manager. For both of us, mentors have had a significant impact on our careers and our lives.

- **Define a career path.** Your organization may, or may not, have a formal career path program. Regardless, it's important to know where you want to be in order to decide how you plan to get there. Where do you want to be in five, 10, and 15 years? What skills will be required to meet those milestones? To consider these desires so early in one's career provides a path that allows you to stay focused and determined. Actions can be taken, and opportunities weighed, to ensure that you get to where you want to be in your professional career. Stay engaged and motived, and remain hyper-vigilant of the education you are receiving each day you step into your office or that of your clients.

Advice to Experienced Sellers

As an experienced seller, you may be noticing new approaches companies are taking to accommodate the influx of eager new sellers. Though a great deal of time and attention have been paid to learn how best to engage this talent pool, there are many benefits for you to take advantage of, as well. With organizations becoming more generationally fluent and flexible, the more seasoned and experienced sellers are also finding ways to provide value during this transition. These ideas are directed toward sellers with several good years of experience under their belts.

Be a Team Player

Share your stories, successes, and failures. New sellers want to hear these valuable lessons and learn from you. At the end of the day, you will probably find that it is easier to be a team player instead of a force of resistance. You may actually enjoy the process, too. Many experienced sellers find it especially rewarding to help people starting out, and your manager will appreciate it more than you can imagine. Wouldn't you have liked to have the opportunity to learn from someone else's experience when you were starting out? This is especially relevant for sellers who aspire to advance to management positions as a next step in their career path.

Be an Educator on Your Generation

If you are an experienced seller representing the Millennial, Gen X, or Baby Boomer generation, think of ways to tactfully understand how to communicate with and sell to individuals from your same generation. You have a unique, inherent perspective into how they see the world, one that is often hard for a seller from another generation to fully comprehend.

Start a Multigenerational Networking Group

Multigenerational networking groups could be set up either within your company or externally with other sales professionals. The concept is to get a group of like-minded people together from each generation to discuss how generational differences are impacting your profession. Technically, all sellers could set up this type of networking group, though sellers with more experience will have more examples and potentially a larger network to leverage when they start the conversation. Consider borrowing ideas from this book as a starting point, but continue to look for evidence of generational nuances impacting your daily interactions. Once sellers know what to look for, and how to potentially overcome these obstacles, it makes the dialogue within the group very dynamic. It is a great way to learn from others and share ideas that help generations understand one another on a more personal level. This translates quickly into success both internally, among colleagues, and on sales visits, as elevated awareness can lead to immediate application.

Become a Mentor

We have already discussed the importance of formal mentorship, but as an experienced seller, you have the option to not wait to be asked. Step up and help your company develop the next crop of talent. You wanted the same things when you started, and it is important to give back. Also, consider reverse mentoring. Popularized by former GE chairman Jack Welsh, reverse mentoring has been around for about a decade but seems to be picking up with the increasingly fast pace of technology in business.

This type of program empowers emerging and established leaders by closing the knowledge gap for both parties. A perfect example could be a younger seller teaching a more experienced seller how to build a LinkedIn profile and use the social media tool for customer prospecting. Through this process, the less experienced seller receives inadvertent skill development. Business acumen tends to rise, and the younger mentor feels valued and a heightened level of professional satisfaction. We see examples of reverse mentoring often in big firms and, though it may feel odd to some more seasoned sales professionals, it can have extremely powerful outcomes when structured properly.

$$\bullet \ \bullet \ \bullet \ \bullet \ \bullet \ \bullet \ \bullet$$

We could fill pages giving advice and recommendations to both new and tenured sellers but when it comes to generational differences, there are three key points to keep in mind:

1. Be aware.

2. Be observant.

3. Adjust.

These three simple steps will help you neutralize generational nuances and make the best out of otherwise challenging selling circumstances. Our hope is that sales leaders have also read this chapter and have gained some insight into how they can help the sellers on their teams be more successful in their roles. In the next chapter, we will spend some time devoted to sales leaders, as they have the difficult task of balancing generational differences and with a multitude of other responsibilities. Let's transition to focusing on the craft of leading high-performing sales teams in today's multigenerational work environment.

9

A Message to
Sales Leaders

"That which seems the height of absurdity in one generation often becomes the height of wisdom in another."

—Adlai Stevenson, American vice president (1835–1914)

This chapter is dedicated to those of you responsible for making sure your team "hits the number." You lead the charge, you set the tone, and it is you who must balance organizational goals while managing your team members' personal and professional aspirations. Sales leadership is not for the faint of heart and can be a "survival of the fittest" experiment for those who take on the challenge.

Meet our friend Keith. He is a sales leader who manages a team of 18 sellers calling on strategic accounts. Keith has more than 15 years of leadership experience, prior to which he carried his own "bag" in a seller role. Keith is a Gen X sales leader with many visible generational tendencies. For example, he is very outspoken, pragmatic, and results-oriented; has a sharp tone when he has strong feelings about something; and can be very bothered by a "we have always done it this way" mentality. He manages mostly Baby Boomer sellers primarily interacting with Millennial colleagues. Keith spends a great deal of time managing change and conflict related to the current demands of the business.

To balance the changing demands of his business, Keith has determined that a multigenerational sales team would likely accelerate his success. He knows that new sellers are required to interact with the current decision makers because he has observed countless sales calls. Sellers with less attachment to the past and recent relevant success are going to carry the business forward faster and interact better with internal and external teams. The organization is changing; business drivers are evolving and decision-makers are struggling with a multitude of competing priorities. Keith knows that business as usual is not an option and quickly got on the move, adding the right sales talent and closely monitoring other sellers. As you've learned throughout the book, there may be obvious challenges to having a multigenerational sales team, but there can be major benefits as well.

A friend of the firm who leads sales effectiveness for Bank of America, Kenneth Burton, told us that "most just assume that leaders won't use everyone's best talents and abilities. We wanted to turn that on its head and be sure to leverage each person's strengths." Good sales leaders are looking for ways to make their people more productive; the best sales leaders have already begun to leverage the concept of Generational Flexibility to make it happen.

Moving the Sales Needle

As part of our work with our clients, we lead a handful of engagements each year focused on sales leadership and coaching. There is a universal theme across most organizations: sales leaders always wish they had more time in the field to develop the talent on their team. This always forces us to ask the question, "What gets in the way?"

The answer comes in the form of both internal and external forces, which tend to distract sales leaders from focusing on what's most important: building the team they need to win. Internally, sales leaders must fight to obtain resources, partner with other departments, manage the needs of their team, and meet management expectations, all while conducting interviews and participating in ongoing corporate initiatives. Because we both have been team leaders ourselves, we appreciate the challenges that the various demands place on sales leaders.

Externally, sales leaders spend time fighting fires that they have little control over but that still burn valuable time from the clock. Industry and regulatory pressures, increased competition, customer complaints, and a rebounding labor market willing to poach top talent make it difficult for sales leaders to do their job and hit their goals. Most sales leaders say that they feel as though they are constantly playing "catch-up," leading us to deduce that sales management is one of the most difficult jobs within many sales organizations.

It's clear that great sales leaders are hard to find, and the turnover in roles like these tends to be high. As a result, organizations will often promote star sellers into managerial roles without considering the different skills sets required for a seller and sales manager. Research from Chally on first-time sales leaders, as well as from a number of organizations, validates this. Promoting ex-superstar sales reps into leadership roles is only successful 15 percent of the time; 85 percent of the time this decision ends in a failed sales leader.[1] It may be a presumed natural career progression, but this internal recruitment practice often falls short, resulting in a loss of talent. Here are a few ideas for how to be more effective as a sales leader, particularly when managing a multigenerational sales team.

• •

Driving Performance

Create an Inclusive Environment

Be more inclusive by building a "we are all in this together" mentality. Employing different generations can be disruptive, for many of the reasons we have discussed thus far. Sales leaders should watch for situations in which the generations may be forming cliques among one another. If you do observe this, make efforts to overemphasize the benefits of working well as one cohesive unit. From troubleshooting generationally charged discord between buyers and sellers, to gaining perspective for the motivations of a fellow colleague from a different generation, creating an inclusive environment can begin the culture shift required to maximize the benefit of a multigenerational team.

Consider a team in which the Millennials, already feeling ostracized, form their own autonomous team. What happens when members of this group begin struggling to prospect and penetrate new accounts? The inabilities of part of the team will undoubtedly impact the team overall. This impact is felt even more when compensation plans involve a team goal component. A team of more experienced sellers provide a great opportunity for these younger Millennial sellers. By providing guidance and helping the Millennials overcome this hurdle, the broader team benefits.

It is one thing to create an environment in which your team is collaborating and assisting one another. It is an entirely different thing to build a transparent culture that perpetuates a sense of ownership and belonging. Alan Powell, an experienced sales leader, told us that "over-communication of business opportunities and challenges within the organization is critical. Even if the team disagrees with the way in which the organization has decided to operate, they understand why the decision was made and appreciate over-communication in lieu of no communication." Inclusiveness is not asking the teams for input on everything and creating such democracy that people become confused about who is in charge. Inclusiveness is creating an atmosphere in which a team understands the goals, understands the challenges, and each person knows what is expected of them. What comes from this is a natural inclination to help one another achieve these goals.

Keep Tabs on Seller Attitudes

Sales roles can quickly feel repetitive and mundane—or worse, draining—especially if people hang up on you or tell you no, day-in and day-out. Great managers should recognize when sellers become disengaged with the role and find ways to reshape what the seller does daily.

A more senior seller may not need that "pick me up" motivational speech but could be reminded of how critical their role is to the health of the organization. Companies want and need experienced sellers to handle high-profile accounts, and sometimes these sellers just need to be reminded of their importance or given extra assignments and roles that engage them. Certainly in sales there's no mistaking the ultimate measure of performance: achieving one's sales targets. However, we have met plenty of successful sellers who continually achieve their targets, but are "burned out" and looking for additional challenges without moving into a formal leadership role. In one case, a top-performing seller coordinated a customer advisory board that included customers from across the business, not just her territory. Another sales team leveraged their most experienced sellers for peer coaching as part of its sales new hire program and provided these sellers with additional incentives related to the success of their new hires.

A new seller may need to understand the importance of gaining sales experience and customer knowledge before being considered for bigger roles within the company. They should understand the paths to success, and the experiences and career paths of other successful sellers on the team. What made them successful? As a leader, you know what makes someone effective, or ineffective, in their role in your business. By discussing an individual's career path, managers can create a more open and inviting forum by which sellers can share their current feelings and desires for the future. By identifying seller competencies, a leader can help the seller navigate the first quarters (or years, depending on sales cycles) by establishing a personal career path that puts them in a good position for success and advancement. This not only benefits the leader but is also greatly appreciated by sellers, with most becoming more engaged and motivated.

In sales, there are often more tough days than celebratory ones, so maintaining a positive outlook is typically a full-time job for many sales leaders, who understand the cyclicality of most selling environments. Helping sellers manage these ups and downs is a critical component of a seller's ability to weather the storm and ensure a long, successful career in sales.

Drive Self-Awareness

From time to time, you will encounter sellers with certain generational quirks. If gone unchecked, these tendencies may lead to lower performance of the seller and potentially the overall team. As their leader, you are charged with recognizing these habits, having the hard conversations, and addressing them head-on. Great leaders make people aware, in a professional way, by holding up a mirror and showing them how their behavior can impact their success or the success of their internal colleagues and customers. Let's say you have a Millennial seller using Snapchat every 30 minutes. As the manager, you have an opportunity to have an honest conversation about productivity in the workplace. The conversation may go like this: "I do not mind if you check your social media while at work; I understand it can be a rather effective prospecting tool. But if it's up on your computer screen, or phone, every time I walk by your desk, I have to assume you aren't being as productive as you could be."

This concept reminds us of a Gen X senior leader who was very well respected but who also had a few very distinct Gen X quirks. First, he was highly opinionated and did not understand the concept of "inner thoughts." Second, he excelled at using expletives in various settings. Third, he was too informal with senior sales leaders, and when his professional style was challenged, he chalked it up to "Well, this is how I roll."

Aside from the leader's own self-sabotage, these detrimental quirks needed to be addressed and corrected, given their impact on the broader organization. The broader team was generationally diverse and his quirks rubbed some the wrong way, especially more tenured Baby Boomers and Millennials. The quirks were seen as inappropriate, unprofessional, and creating an environment that cheapened things for other employees. At many levels, this behavior does not help the leader or anyone around them, and has likely driven away many people who may not have spoken up on the way out.

Even those sellers who have been in the game for a while often need slight course corrections. One such course correction involved a Baby Boomer seller who, on sales calls, would say to younger decision-makers, "I have been doing this a really long time—longer than most of you can imagine." It would normally set people off when he constantly referenced how things used to be "back in the day." These easily coached behaviors may put you in an uncomfortable position, but correcting them is part of the job.

Stay Engaged to Stay Relevant

Even in the craziest of times, it is important to have a network of other sales leaders you can collaborate with, internally and externally, to expand your thinking. Consider engaging sales leaders from other generations who can help you solve for issues that may require generational adaptation. For example, a sales leader may struggle to relate to someone on their team because of the generational divide. This is a great time to connect with a leader from that generation.

At the end of a recent breakfast speech on the topic of generational selling, a Baby Boomer sales professional approached David with a classic example of this exact issue. She works in an office located in Manhattan's Financial District and has an associate who lives well south of the city. It takes him 90 minutes, each way, to get to work. She described the associate as a highly effective Millennial and a bright star whom she wants to keep engaged in her business. The associate asked her for some flexibility on Fridays. By working from home, the Millennial could avoid sitting in traffic and maximize the amount of time he spent working.

This Baby Boomer, unfamiliar with the advantages Millennials find as it relates to workplace flexibility, cited her concern for how productive individuals who "work from home" can be. I asked her, "Do you want to keep this employee?" She immediately said, "Yes. He is so productive. I am worried that if I do not show some flexibility I could lose him." In the end, she decided to offer up some flexibility and allowed the Millennial to work from home on Fridays. As a trade-off, she will closely manage productivity on these days. There was enough generational variety among her team that she could quickly see that she needed to adjust her thinking to relate to this Millennial shining star. When asking for help from others, make sure to bring concrete examples for discussion so that you can be clear about the advice you need. This was a great example of a real need and a leader asking for specific advice.

. . . .

Building Your Case for Change

Building a high-performing team takes an incredible amount of effort and should be considered a long-term initiative. Likely not achieved after a few training sessions, this process could take years.

A long-term client of Symmetrics Group has achieved a stable leadership team accompanied by very low turnover among its sellers. It has multiple offices covering the United States, Canada, and Australia. This client has been on a steady growth trajectory, and the sales leadership team has led a very robust program to develop and retain talent. They have developed and deployed the full "Way of Sales" model (as described in Chapter 4), done assessments for people to better understand unique thinking preferences, run closing skills and negotiating skills training, conducted key account training, executed full account plans, completed leadership development sessions, and built a comprehensive onboarding program for new hire sellers. As you can imagine, this well-oiled machine was not developed overnight; instead, they have made a true commitment to building a high-performing sales team over time. Each of these strategies could have some degree of generational nuances in the mix based on the generations of their sellers and of those they serve. Newer sellers, in this case, have welcomed all of the training, while some of the more tenured sellers have shown fatigue with the constant focus on talent development. Every time they embark on a new initiative, the leaders spend time trying to figure out how to position the content in a way that engages the whole team and drives the desired outcomes.

As a leader, it is important to decide whether minor tweaks are required to address generational diversity or if more sweeping, wholesale changes are required. In our previous book, *7 Steps to Sales Force Transformation*, we assist sales leaders looking to enact change and help them diagnose what is required to successfully bring that change to fruition. Let's take a look at each of the seven steps, considering the changes organizations can make to support generational diversity.

Step 1: What Is Driving the Need for Change?

Before making any changes to address generational nuances, you must understand the root causes of the generational friction you are experiencing. For example, are you experiencing difficulties caused by generational differences within your current sales team, in customer interactions, or both? To the extent a sales leader sees friction within their current sales team, they should consider asking themselves the following questions:

- Is the friction a random, one-off occurrence, or is it a trend?

- When did you first observe the friction, and are you sure you understand the full story?

- Are some sellers struggling with generational differences more than others?

- Is the friction just social, or is it also professional—meaning, it is affecting the way they are getting work done and engaging with coworkers?

- What is at stake (e.g., engagement, productivity, overall job satisfaction, demotivating the remainder of the team, etc.)?

Let's say a sales leader suspects issues within customer interactions. Consider the same questions, just through a slightly different lens:

- Is the friction a random, one-off occurrence, or is it a trend?

- When did you first observe the friction, and are you sure you understand the full story?

- Are some of your sellers or buyers struggling with generational differences more than others?

- Is the friction just social, or is it also professional—meaning, it is affecting the willingness of your customer to spend money or continue services with your company?

- What is at stake (e.g., revenue, productivity, customer retention, customer satisfaction, etc.)?

Once a leader nails the root causes and determines what behaviors need to change, they can progress to Step 2.

Step 2: What Does Your Sales Vision Look Like?

As you think about the future, how do you see generational nuances impacting your short-term and long-term sales strategy? Identifying future implications, likely to impact the sales organization if not addressed, provides perspective and a starting point by which leaders can define a path forward. For example, what if your sales organization requires a substantial change in the organizational structure in order to more effectively utilize inside sales reps to maintain a specific subset of customers? This change triggers the need to recruit a less-tenured team of sellers who can deal with being on the phone all day long as they develop skills and industry knowledge. The leader would be recommending a well-developed inside sales structure, including onboarding, training, and ongoing development of new sellers.

Does this change involve generational considerations? Yes! The new sellers will likely be Millennials with minimal sales experience. This influx of new talent, required to meet the specific needs of the inside sales department, will inevitably change the culture of the overall sales organization immediately and require sales leaders to brace for impact.

Step 3: What Is Your Case for Change?

Think of this step as defining the internal campaign, or value proposition, for why effort should be applied. Leaders may receive some resistance from others within the organization. Creating a vision for a topic not considered "mission critical" could create some push-back from more numbers-oriented and results-oriented leaders. An internal campaign will likely take the collective efforts of many people. When considering an effort to minimize generational flare-ups, you will likely include HR and marketing. A well-crafted internal campaign will clearly state the problems, why they need to be addressed, the primary benefits (internally and externally), the expected outcomes, and how this will position a company differently in the market or in the face of the generational transformation. This critical step can't be sold short, especially if a request for resources, time, and money is required.

Step 4: What Support Do You Need to Succeed?

Once you've developed your internal campaign, you should determine who you need to get on board to support your efforts. We wrote in *7 Steps to Sales Force Transformation*, "A sales transformation needs cross-functional support to have the highest chance of success."[2] The reality is that if in sales you are experiencing challenges caused by generational nuances, the likelihood is that other departments are feeling similar challenges as well. Seeking out to what extent other parts of the organization are experiencing similar generational tension may help get the support you need. By creating a "we are all in this boat together" mentality, organization alignment increases. Use tangible examples and pieces of your campaign to get the right conversations started. We once delivered a session on presentation skills for an audience of senior leaders. When we began discussing the next generation of leaders, one of the key people in the room said, "Look around. We are all old. There are no plans for who is taking over. Who is going to run this business in the next 10 to

15 years? Don't ask me!" Immediately, our burning platform was apparent and the team immediately realized that this conversation needed to expand. Soon it included stakeholders from human resources, marketing, sales, and local leadership in key U.S. markets. When making your case for change, it's always important to consider the audience in order to determine what other stakeholders can help you make your case.

Step 5: How Are You Going to Get There?

The key to making any change a success is having a road map that is understood and agreed upon by all relevant stakeholders and impacted parties. This road map must sequence major milestones in a logical and impactful way, while recognizing that "planning and preparation are important, but you often learn more by using a process of intelligent iteration than developing endless plans."[3] Engaging stakeholders could lead to so many opinions that you run the risk of getting stuck. Avoid getting stuck in analysis paralysis by making a plan that is logical and well-communicated, and be sure your review cadence is well-established to ensure adjustments are made as needed.

Consider this example: Let's say that a company realizes that to sustain future growth, it will need to reshape the role of direct sellers to transition from a product-oriented focus to more solution-oriented. To make matters more complex, 70 percent of their sales team will be retiring in the next 10 years. There is a real chance that some people on the support team could say, "Let's not worry about this right now. We have 10 years before we have to push the panic button." The reality is, you do not have 10 years! Without a robust sales force to backfill the exodus of top talent, sales and revenue will falter. What's a company to do?

In this case, a plan might call for new job descriptions, a phased recruitment and hiring of new sellers, reshaped roles, onboarding, coaching, mentoring, and ongoing feedback intended to capture learnings and best practices along the way. Each component of the plan should be assigned to an individual designated to lead the charge. With a regular review cadence, the accountable individual will provide an overview of key learnings and milestone achievements. Tangible progress against a plan will help to keep people bought in to the transformation and helps leaders avoid the "flavor of the month" feeling that often occurs given competing priorities. With the completion of each component, the plan gains momentum and continues to be credentialed.

Step 6: What Do You Have to Do to Put Your Plans Into Action?

This is where all of the great planning is put into action. We have seen many great plans go no further than the conference room wall, never fully deployed due to a variety of reasons. Maybe a new product launch became the focus or a reshaping of sales territories. Maybe a new leadership team decided to focus on key account strategies or merging a recent acquisition.

There are dozens of reasons why a plan to address generational issues could get left on the conference room walls as other things get chased. Measuring success—even minor goals—is important to making sure you continue to make progress. Leaders of great change efforts identify quick wins and highlight them to others involved so that they can see where and how incremental progress is made. Let's continue the example from Step 5, in which 70 percent of the sales team will retire in 10 years. The company has successfully added four new Millennial sellers who fit the mold required to ensure the vision for the future becomes a reality. Sales leaders have been in the field coaching them and observing performance on sales calls. The sales leaders have started to identify the strength of these new sellers alongside skill and knowledge gaps. This is the time to communicate clearly and lock in the recruiting profile, development plans, and sales skill development requirements. This is where sales leaders must be held accountable for driving the necessary adjustments in order to ensure momentum is not lost.

Step 7: How Do You Realize Our Return on Investment?

Great transformations don't just happen with a strong up-front plan or a "big bang" start. Your efforts and investment must be sustained throughout the duration of the change initiative. There should be just as much excitement throughout your initiative as there is at the beginning. To help accomplish this, revisit your story or case for change (developed in Step 3) regularly. Remind people why making changes that accommodate generational differences is important and what is at stake for establishing the right behaviors.

If your plan is well-developed, then it will include key activities and goals that have clear metrics, though not everything you do in a generational transformation needs to be measured. For example, arming people with better knowledge of how generational differences may impact sales overall is tough to measure. However, there are some things you *can*, and should, measure and report as ROI related to the change efforts. Measurable items could include:

- Number of new hires fitting the desired profile.
- Ramp of new sellers (time to productivity) and how this has trended over time.
- Number of field coaching interactions by sales leaders to address generational nuances.
- Quota attainment, by generation.
- Client retention and portfolio growth stats, by generation.
- Employee engagement survey data (before and after major change initiative).
- Exit and "stay" interview or focus group intelligence, by generation.
- Voice of the customer feedback.

Having these types of measurable data points available helps leaders gain the ongoing support and resources required for future change initiatives. Leaders who closely manage ROI will always have a better track record of tangible results that translate to success. This is just smart planning and fact-based performance management.

• • • • • • •

The role of a sales leader will never be easy, but we truly hope we have offered some practical ideas and tips for building a strong multi-generational sales team. Sales leaders are uniquely positioned to deal with generational nuances affecting their business, which is why we believe it is so critical to own the required knowledge and be open to gaining more Generational Flexibility. Now is the time to create an environment in which more sellers and sales leaders can thrive in their careers.

Welcome to the Future

> "There is no more reason to think that they expected the world to remain static than there is to think that any of us holds a crystal ball. The only way to create a foundational document that could stand the test of time was to build in enough flexibility that later generations would be able to adapt it to their own needs and uses."
>
> —Diane Wood, Chief Judge of the United States Court of Appeals for the Seventh Circuit (1950–)

Let's imagine it is now 2025. Though we are far from prognosticators, we feel the dynamics of the workforce currently look a little something like this:

- Baby Boomers continue to be the smallest segment of the workforce, their numbers dwindling at a rapid pace.

- Gen X is a shrinking demographic as senior sellers and leaders are preparing for retirement.

- Seventy-five percent of the U.S. workforce is Millennials, many having entered leadership positions and gaining substantial experience. They, too, have now "paid their dues."

These now-tenured Millennials are forced to cope with the next generation entering the professional workplace. Generation Z is taking a stronghold in those entry-level positions once reserved for, well, every generation that came before. The cycle is beginning anew.

It has been eight years since we first published *The Multigenerational Sales Team*. With millions of copies sold, we have heard firsthand the power of Generational Flexibility from the perspective of organizations, individual sellers, and sales leaders. Preferences for communication styles, technology, work/life balance, and personal motivators are continuing to evolve, as they have since the industrial revolution, and many of the characteristics that define each generation are also shifting beneath our very feet. This will require even the most progressive organizations, and individuals alike, to be conscious of changing buyer behaviors, recruiting protocols, effective onboarding practices, and the power of personalized coaching and development through the lens of generational diversity.

As we look back at the progression of professional selling during the past 50 years, we see advances in each of these areas and have met many top performers who seem to demonstrate a mastery for it all. The core skills of a successful seller have not necessarily changed all that much, but we would argue that a successful seller in 2025 knows how to limit the impacts of generational differences by being aware and observant, and by adjusting their behavior.

We will now leave it to our Millennial readers to update the examples and concepts from this book as their insights and knowledge will inevitably shape the next successful multigenerational sales team.

Notes

Introduction

1. Marston, Cam. Generational Insights website. *https://generationalinsights.com* (2016).

Chapter 1

1. Starbucks website. *www.starbucks.com/about-us/company-information*.

2. "Labor Force Statistics From the Current Population Survey." *www.bls.gov/cps/cpsaat03.htm* (2015).

3. Kessler, Glenn. "Do 10,000 Baby Boomers Retire Every Day?" *Washington Post. www.washingtonpost.com* (July 24, 2014).

4. Twaronite, Karyn. "Global Generations—A Global Study on Work-Life Challenges Across Generations." EY website. *www.ey.com* (2015).

5. Allman, Steven. "Job Hopping Stigma Changes: Since 1960, Average Tenure on the Job Reduced by More Than 18 Years." *Star-News. https://news.google.com/newspapers* (March 156, 2003).

6.   "Bureau of Labor Statistics: Employee Tenure Summary."
     Bureau of Labor Statistics website. *www.bls.gov/news.release/
     tenure.nr0.htm* (September 2014).

7.   *www.u-s-history.com/pages/h980.html.*

8.   Bureau of Labor Statistics. "A Century of Change: The U.S.
     Labor Force, 1950–2050." Bureau of Labor Statistics website.
     www.bls.gov/opub/mlr/2002/05/art2full.pdf (May 2002).

9.   Common Business-Oriented Language, a computer
     programming language.

10. Lewis, Michael. *The New New Thing: A Silicon Valley Story*
     (W.W. Norton & Company, 2014).

11. "The Creed of Speed: Is the Pace of Business Really Getting
     Quicker?" *The Economist. www.economist.com/news/
     briefing/21679448-pace-business-really-getting-quicker-creed-
     speed* December 5, 2015).

12. Ibid.

13. The Council of Economic Advisers. "15 Economic Facts
     About Millennials." The White House website.
     *www.whitehouse.gov/sites/default/files/docs/millennials_
     report.pdf* (October, 2014).

14. "One-Third of Companies Have Missed Revenue
     Goals in the Last Year—CareerBuilder and Indiana
     University's Kelley School of Business Launch Moneyball
     to Help Companies Improve Sales Performance."
     CareerBuilder website. *www.careerbuilder.es/share/aboutus/
     pressreleasesdetail.aspx?sd=6%2F20%2F2013&id=pr765&ed=
     12%2F31%2F2013* (June 20, 2013).

15. "IU Kelley School of Business and CareerBuilder Form
     Strategic Partnership to Deliver Training Online."
     http://newsinfo.iu.edu/news/page/normal/23423.html
     (June 11, 2013).

16. "One-Third of Companies."

17. Healthgrades website. *www.healthgrades.com/about.*

Chapter 2

1. "2015 Central Garden and Pet Annual Report."
    http://ir.central.com/Annual_Reports.

2. Adapted from "Generational Differences Chart." West
    Midland Family Center website. *www.wmfc.org/uploads/
    GenerationalDifferencesChart.pdf.*

3. Goodreads website. *www.goodreads.com/quotes/14793-every-
    generation-imagines-itself-to-be-more-intelligent-than-the.*

4. "Most Millennials Resist the 'Millennial' Label." Pew
    Research Center. *www.people-press.org/2015/09/03/most-
    millennials-resist-the-millennial-label* (September 3, 2015).

5. Fry, Richard. "For Millennials, a Bachelor's Degree
    Continues to Pay Off, but a Master's Earns Even More." Pew
    Research Center. *www.pewresearch.org/fact-tank/2014/02/28/
    for-millennials-a-bachelors-degree-continues-to-pay-off-but-
    a-masters-earns-even-more* (February 28, 2014).

6. Fry, Richard. "For First Time in Modern Era, Living With
    Parents Edges Out Other Living Arrangements for 18- to
    34-Year-Olds." Pew Research Center. *www.pewsocialtrends.
    org/2016/05/24/for-first-time-in-modern-era-living-with-
    parents-edges-out-other-living-arrangements-for-18-to-34-
    year-olds* (May 24, 2016).

7. "Most Millennials Resist the 'Millennial' Label." Pew
    Research Center. *www.people-press.org* (September 3, 2015;
    retrieved August 15, 2016).

8. The TRACOM Group website. *http://tracomcorp.com.*

9. This section was inspired by VorsightBP's excellent research
    paper "Mythbusting Millennials: Separating Fact From
    Fiction for Managing Gen Y Sales Reps." Retrieved from
    http://sales.vorsightbp.com/ebook-mythbusting-millennials.

10. Giang, Vivian. "Top 5 Reasons Gen X Workers Quit Their
    Jobs." American Express website. *www.american express.com*
    (January 17, 2013).

11. Asghar, Rob. "Study: Millennials' Work Ethic Is in the Eye of the Beholder." *Forbes. www.forbes.com/sites/robasghar/2014/01/29/study-millennials-work-ethic-is-in-the-eye-of-the-beholder/#1f0b78f93768* (January 29, 2014).

12. Gani, Aisha. "Millennials at Work: Five Stereotypes—and Why They Are (Mostly) Wrong." *The Guardian. www.theguardian.com/world/2016/mar/15/millennials-work-five-stereotypes-generation-y-jobs* (March 15, 2016).

13. "Generation X Not So Special: Malaise, Cynicism on the Rise for All Age Groups." Stanford University news release. *news.stanford.edu/pr/98/980821genx.html.*

14. "Slacker [Def. 1]." *Merriam-Webster* Online. *www.merriam-webster.com/dictionary/slacker* (retrieved August 15, 2016).

15. Taylor, Paul, and George Gao. "Generation X: America's Neglected 'Middle Child'." Pew Research Center. *www.pewresearch.org/fact-tank/2014/06/05/generation-x-americas-neglected-middle-child* (June 5, 2014).

16. Lockard, Pamela. "Should You Market to Baby Boomers on Social Media?" DMN3 website. *www.dmn3.com/dmn3-blog/should-you-market-to-baby-boomers-on-social-media* (February 19, 2016).

17. Abrahms, Sally. "Five Myths About Baby Boomers." *Washington Post. www.washingtonpost.com/opinions/five-myths-about-baby-boomers/2015/11/06/44ca943c-83fb-11e5-8ba6-cec48b74b2a7_story.html?utm_term=.e2f52888663d* (November 6, 2015).

18. Ibid.

19. Stein, Joel. "The Me Me Me Generation—Millennials Are Lazy, Entitled Narcissists Who Still Live With Their Parents." *Time. http://time.com/247/millennials-the-me-me-me-generation* (May 20, 2013).

Chapter 3

1. Rainie, Lee, and Andrew Perrin. "Technology Adoption by Baby Boomers (and Everybody Else)." Pew Research Center. *www.pewinternet.org/2016/03/22/technology-adoption-by-baby-boomers-and-everybody-else/* (March 22, 2106).

2. Numbers in text and in graphics do not always total 100 percent due to rounding,

3. See *www.clearslide.com*.

4. Green, Charlie. *Trust Based Selling.*

Chapter 4

1. Vasquez, Adam, and Heather Wadlinger. "The Next Generation of B2B Buyers: How the Millennial Business Buyer Is Changing B2B Sales & Marketing." Sacunas website. *www.sacunas.net/#/millenial-b2b* (March 2016).

2. "Sales Training." Training Industry Inc. website. *www.trainingindustry.com/wiki/entries/sales-training.aspx.*

3. Adamson, Brent, and Matthew Dixon. *The Challenger Sale: Taking Control of the Customer Conversation* (Penguin, 2011).

4. Collins, James C. *Good to Great: Why Some Companies Make the Leap—and Others Don't* (New York: HarperBusiness, 2001).

Chapter 5

1. Twaronite, Karyn. "Global Generations: A Global Study on Work-Life Challenges Across Generations." EY website. *www.ey.com* (2015).

2. Estis, Ryan. "3 Keys to Leading the Next-Generation Sales Organization." Business 2 Community website. *www.business2community.com/sales-management/3-keys-leading-next-generation-sales-organization-01428156#GzOVedj4b2ebLc5g.97* (January 14, 2016).

3. "Sales Recruiters: How to Hire Top Sales People." Monster.com. *http://hiring.monster.com/hr/hr-best-practices/recruiting-hiring-advice/acquiring-job-candidates/sales-recruitment.aspx.*

Chapter 6

1. "Younger Managers Rise in the Ranks: Survey Quantifies Management Shift and Reveals Challenges, Preferred Workplace Perks, and Perceived Generational Strengths and Weaknesses." EY press release, September 3, 2013. *www.multivu.com/mnr/63068-ernst-and-young-llp-research-younger-managers-rise-in-the-ranks.*

2. "Leveling Up: How to Win in the Skills Economy." Payscale, March 2016.

Chapter 7

1. "Ask Gen-E: I'm a Boomer; My Boss Is 24. What Should I Do?" *Philadelphia Business Journal. www.bizjournals.com/philadelphia/blog/guest-comment/2016/01/ask-gen-e-im-a-boomer-my-boss-is-24-what-should-i.html* (January 15, 2016).

2. Cherry, K. "Common Leadership Styles and When to Use Them." October 5, 2016.

3. Snyder, Benjamin. "Half of Us Have Quit Our Job Because of a Bad Boss." *Fortune. http://fortune.com/2015/04/02/quit-reasons* (April 2, 2015).

4. Dua, Tanya. "Employee Reviews During Manicures: How Millennial Staffers Are Changing Agency Practices." *http://digiday.com/agencies/employee-reviews-manicures-millennial-staffers-changing-agency-practices* (January 13, 2016).

Chapter 8

1. For example profiles of several top performers, see *http://symmetricsgroup.com/big-ideas/top-performers/*.

2. Check out *www.bunnellideagroup.com/#growbig-faster* for more information.

Chapter 9

1. Fisher, Anne. "3 Secrets to Hiring Great Salespeople." *Fortune. http://fortune.com/2016/08/28/hiring-salespeople-tips* (August 28, 2016).

2. Perla and Shiver, *7 Steps*.

3. Ibid.

Index

About the Authors

Warren Shiver is the Founder and Managing Partner of Symmetrics Group, one of America's fastest-growing private companies, which is dedicated to driving sustainable revenue improvements by transforming sales organizations. With more than 20 years of sales, management, and consulting experience working for firms such as Accenture, OnTarget, and North Highland, Warren has helped establish Symmetrics Group as a go-to company for organizations that desire to transform the way their sales teams function. Warren holds an MBA from Duke University and a bachelor's in Mechanical Engineering from Georgia Institute of Technology. Warren is the co-author with Michael Perla of *7 Steps to Sales Force Transformation*.

David Szen is a Principal Consultant with Symmetrics Group. In this role, he helps to lead sales transformations and train and coach sales teams and leaders. He brings more than 25 years of sales, sales management, sales effectiveness consulting, workshop design and training experience working for firms such as Cox Target Media, Valpak, and Crown Marketing Group. David has frontline experience leading sales teams and selling at the strategic level, which helps him bring reality into everything he does. David holds a BS in Marketing from State University of New York at Buffalo.